Set Margins' #80

Printed with the support of
the Graham Foundation for Advanced Studies in the Fine Arts
and Stimuleringfonds (The Creative Industries Fund NL)

They asked me to design a house, *I asked them to design a home*

Beyond the Architectural House
Reflections and Exercises on Domestic Life

Edited by
Ilaria Palmieri & Georgina Pantazopoulou

Published by
Set Margins'

To those who design and take care of spaces despite the obstacle and who push through tight budgets, deadlines, and moments of doubt because they believe their work matters.

To everyone balancing work, worry, and the drive to imagine something better. You are the ones who still believe it is worth imagining houses differently.

To those who keep making, building, and dreaming – even in exhaustion, even when recognition feels far away – your persistence is not invisible. And neither is the value of what you create.

This work is for you.

INDEX

INTRODUCTION

Home becomes the impossibility and necessity of the subject's future (one never gets there, but is always getting there), rather than the past which binds the self to a given place.

Sara Ahmed [1]

Welcome.

Do these words catch you off guard? They hint at a truth that can be unsettling: that "home" may not be certain, fixed, or even singular. That there might be both a "home" and an "away" – and that sometimes, home becomes unreachable, while away feels alien and estranged. These words challenge the traditional idea of home as a place of stability, comfort, and safety. Instead, they suggest that home is both a necessity and an impossibility.

What if home isn't something we're simply given, but something we shape through our actions, relationships, and histories? What if home doesn't always mean safety or privacy? What if the place you live in doesn't hold your memories, your creativity, your sense of intimacy? What if, over time, you forgot how to dream there – or to imagine anything at all?

These words suggest that home is not just a physical space but a shifting landscape where identity is constantly in flux. That the act of making home involves both connection and disconnection, comfort and estrangement. And that the feelings we associate with home aren't purely personal – they're shaped by larger cultural, social, and historical forces that influence what it means to belong, or to be cast adrift.

Ultimately, these words invite you to consider a more nuanced, inclusive understanding of home – one that embraces its complexity, its fluidity, and its contradictions.

When we – Ilaria and Georgina – first met among the chairs and desks of our university, beginning a new chapter of life in the Netherlands, we were both searching for a sense of *familiarity* – something to hold onto, far from our home countries, Italy and Greece. In the second year of our Master's in Interior Architecture,

They asked me to design a house,

1
Sara Ahmed, "Home and Away: Narratives of Migration and Estrangement," *International Journal of Cultural Studies 2*, no. 3 (December 1999): 331.

2
Ibid, 341.

3
Ibid.

4
Luce Beeckmans et al., eds., *Making Home(s) in Displacement: Critical Reflections on a Spatial Practice* (Leuven University Press, 2022), 9.

5
Le Corbusier, *The Modulor* (Faber & Faber, 1961).

6
Alison Place, *Feminist Designer: On the Personal and the Political in Design* (MIT Press, 2023), 47.

as we embarked on our graduation projects, we found the space to explore that longing. Through research and design, we began to weave narratives rooted in the very familiarity we had been missing. In doing so, we discovered a set of practices, gestures, and everyday performances that allowed us to connect with our new environment – ways of being that echoed how we had once felt at home. Little did we know that, in our quest to find that familiarity, we needed to understand that "the question of home and being at home can only be addressed by considering the question of affect: being at home is here a matter of how one feels or how one might fail to feel."[2]
Home, we realized, carries its own layers of strangeness and transformation. It is not a static or purely familiar space; rather, it is shaped by movement, by shifts and relocations, forming a complex and continually evolving experience of dwelling. We came to understand that feeling at home is not a fixed state but a lived, ongoing process – one in which the boundaries between self and space blur. It is a relationship in which the individual shapes the space, even as the space, in turn, shapes the individual.[3]
We then began to question how deeply these interconnected aspects of home are considered within spatial practices – the disciplines responsible for defining the physical – as in spatial – dimensions of such relationships. Home is often our first environment – the place where we begin to navigate a microcosm of the broader social and cultural world. It is not defined solely by its physical form, but also by the social norms, values, and stereotypes that inhabit and shape it. Today's spatial and architectural conversation about the notion of home is still based on traditional and idealized associations of "comfort and security"[4] overlooking the spatial and material dynamics involved in shaping a home. Much of contemporary architecture and interior design finds its roots in the modernist era, heavily influenced by concepts such as Le Corbusier's *Modulor*.[5] This approach often followed a "default user" pattern predominantly based on the white, Western, cisgender male.[6] The spatial outcomes of this period, such as the well-known Grete Schütte-Lihotzky's *Frankfurt Kitchen*[7] (1926), emphasized efficiency and practicality, often perpetuated entrenched social norms, prioritizing functional transformation rather than setting the ground for a deeper dialogue about structural emancipation.[8] Such a dialogue could challenge traditional design processes, reimagining how homes are created and how they can contribute to more equitable, inclusive, and ultimately familiar living environments.

7
The design of the Frankfurt Kitchen was inspired by the American home economist Christine Frederick, who applied Frederick W. Taylor's principles of optimizing mass manufacturing efficiency to household tasks. Lihotzky carried out time and motion studies for various cleaning chores in the home. To keep costs down, she chose a modular design measuring 1.9 by 2.4 meters. Each kitchen included a gas stove, a garbage drawer, a foldable ironing board, a swivel stool, and aluminum food containers. Over 10,000 of these kitchens were installed in the housing projects of New Frankfurt. Lihotzky often felt uneasy about her role as the only female architect on the team, realizing that by agreeing to design the kitchen, she had reinforced gender stereotypes and lacked the necessary experience. She wrote in her memoir, *Why I Became an Architect* that unlike many other women, she "never managed a household, cooked, or had any experience in the kitchen whatsoever. [...] Had I known that everyone would only talk about this damned kitchen, I would never have invented it."

8
Leonie Sandercock and Ann Forsyth, "A Gender Agenda: New Directions for Planning Theory," *Journal of The American Planning Association 58*, no. 1 (March 31, 1992): 49–59.

This publication is an effort to reframe the conversation around the notion of home – presenting domesticity as a space that reflects the multidimensional nature of everyday life. We began this research as spatial practitioners who felt the need to develop new tools – or reimagine existing ones – in order to approach the design of domestic spaces differently. How can designers adopt research methods that listen to, collect, and activate voices and behaviours that often go unspoken?
As we spontaneously came together, it felt natural to continue working collaboratively while developing this publication. In these pages, we gather and share observations and stories that reveal the layers and complexities of the space we call home. This collection brings together diverse and meaningful voices – individuals who, through their research and practice, have engaged deeply with the home environment and its design, rethinking conventional approaches and proposing alternatives. But most importantly, most of these voices, like ours, have personally experienced the transition from what we once called home to what we now consider a *re-created home.* Together, we aim to share diverse ways of understanding and creating a domestic space:

Through personal stories and lived experiences;
Through architecture and design practice.

By gathering these narratives, we invite interior architects, designers, readers, practitioners, and thinkers, to collectively discuss the subject of domestic space, reflecting on and re-evaluating current design principles.

Our approach is collaborative, inclusive, and grounded in lived experience, aiming to stay close to the subject we are exploring. Just as the experience of being *at home* involves the "question of affect,"[9] so does the way we write about it. This book aims to be a "collaborative journey"[10] between reader and writer, leading to an "affective"[11] writing rather than only an effective one.[12] This approach helps reveal the relational side of domestic spaces, focusing on the diverse experiences of those who are often underrepresented. We want to offer a more personal perspective, moving away from a traditional academic framework – a space officially recognized as entitled to address such conversations and to produce knowledge – which often remains detached from the experience of the reader.

They asked me to design a house,

9
Ahmed, "Home and Away," 341.

10
Jayne Pitard, "A Journey to the Centre of Self: Positioning the Researcher in Autoethnography | Forum Qualitative Sozialforschung / Forum: Qualitative Social Research," *Forum Qualitative Sozialforschung / Forum: Qualitative Social Research* 18, no. 3 (September 2017).

11
Luce Beeckmans, Ashika Singh, and Alessandra Gola, "Rethinking the Intersection of Home and Displacement from a Spatial Perspective," in *Making Home(s) in Displacement,* ed. Luce Beeckmans et al., Critical Reflections on a Spatial Practice (Leuven University Press, 2022), 27.

12
Ibid.

Embracing a personal perspective helps us bridge an interdisciplinary approach that can cultivate a dynamic and productive environment where individuals from diverse cultural backgrounds and contexts can learn from each other,[13] contributing a variety of perspectives to the inherently multilayered subject of domesticity.

But, we need to say,

The role that domesticity plays in our daily lives is often overlooked. In architecture, it is frequently regarded as a minor or less valuable area of intervention. At the same time, an ongoing discussion between the fields of architecture and interior architecture/design continues to unfold around the design of the home environment. Interior architects and designers are uniquely positioned to engage with this domain – their education and practice centre on spatial interiority and its relationship to the human – and, at times, more-than-human – experience.

Architecture as a discipline also addresses domesticity, with house design forming part of both its academic curriculum and professional trajectory. However, the ways in which these trajectories engage with domesticity are shaped by deeper historical and ideological frameworks – frameworks that influence how value is assigned to domestic space and who is seen as responsible for shaping it.

The relationship between architecture and domesticity is far from neutral. Even today, architectural pedagogy often remains rooted in the principles of modernism, with emphasis on rationality and universal principles, often disregarding domestic spaces as sites of subjective experience. As a result, the field's foundational narratives have historically marginalized domesticity, reinforcing a masculine-coded identity that continues to shape architectural discourse today. The emergence of the domestic ideal was deeply tied to the rise of industrial capitalism and imperialism.[14] Domesticity was constructed alongside these socio-economic transformations, becoming a reflection of shifting social structures and cultural ideals. These historical developments framed domestic spaces as sites where gender roles[15] were both performed and reinforced – aligning femininity[16] with the private sphere of home and care, while masculinity remained linked to the public realm of industry and public life.[17]

Even if the field of interior design, which includes domesticity, is today officially recognized in educational and professional

13
Laura Sanderson and Sally Stone, eds., *Emerging Practices in Architectural Pedagogy: Accommodating an Uncertain Future* (Abingdon: Routledge, 2021), 6.

14
Gülsüm Baydar and Hilde Heynen, *Negotiating Domesticity: Spatial Productions of Gender in Modern Architecture* (Abingdon: Routledge, 2005), 6.

15
See also: Dolores Hayden, *The Grand Domestic Revolution: A History of Feminist Designs for American Homes, Neighborhoods, and Cities* (Cambridge, MA: MIT Press, 2000).

16
Bart Verschaffel, "The Meanings of Domesticity," *The Journal of Architecture 7,* no. 3 (2002): 287–96; Witold Rybczynski, *Home: A Short History of an Idea* (New York: Penguin Books, 1987), 51–75.

17
Baydar and Heynen, *Negotiating Domesticity,* 6.

contexts, it continues to be socially associated with female figures. Furthermore, how many care-related practices, which conventionally fall within the domestic sphere and are culturally assigned to women, continue to be overlooked? They are countless. While the role of interior designers may be acknowledged in spatial education, the importance of domesticity in daily life remains insufficiently valued on a broader scale within the field. It didn't come as a surprise for us that the sociological, cultural and philosophical worlds[18] face the topics of the domestic with a much more honest, inclusive, all-considered perspective that the spatial design has done so far. Space, as Doreen Massey notes, is not static; it is socially produced and always under construction, intersecting with power relations, gender, and class.[19] This research aims to bring these dynamics to the forefront, emphasizing their importance in the design of domestic spaces, while also questioning conventional approaches to how knowledge is shared and utilized within the design process of it.[20] We ground our work in a feminist perspective, specifically an intersectional feminist framework that considers the intersections of gender, age, race, class, and cultural and geographical context. This book builds on this foundation, bringing together diverse voices to explore design interactions across three interconnected dimensions: the personal, the community, and the institutional.[21] We believe these exact three levels are the ones that are intricately intertwined, overlaid within the domestic environment, shaping and being shaped by the relations that unfold within it. Yet, these dimensions are often overlooked in the design process.

As female designers, architects, and writers, we believe that an intersectional feminist approach to the domestic environment can provide alternative ways of understanding the conditions under which projects are formulated and the processes through which design really works.[22] Gender-sensitive pedagogies encourage the recognition of diversity and difference, while feminist pedagogies highlight our interconnectedness, emphasizing the importance of sharing, redistributing resources, and striving for the collective good rather than merely pursuing individual goals.[23] The words, conversations, illustrations that you will encounter in these pages put emphasis on collaboration, cross-disciplinary exchange, contingency, and the belief that if the sphere of the design of the domestic is to play an incisive role in the broader spatial discipline, we must reconsider the way "architectural knowledge is produced and

18
Alexa Winton, "Inhabited Space: Critical Theories and the Domestic Interior," in *The Handbook of Interior Architecture and Design,* ed. Lois Weinthal and Graeme Brooker (London and New York: Bloomsbury, 2013), 40–49.

19
Doreen Massey, *Space, Place and Gender* (Cambridge: Polity Press, 2007), 2.

20
A great inspiration for our research and practice is Phyllis Birkby's "Herspace" (1970s). In this project, she brought together a group of women to collaboratively design their home environments, using drawing and writing as shared language. This collective approach not only cultivated mutual inspiration throughout the design process, but also unearthed knowledge and insights that might have otherwise remained hidden. See also: Phyllis Birkby, "Herspace," *Making Room: Women and Architecture* 3, no. 3 (1981): 28–29.

21
Sasha Costanza-Chock, *Design Justice: Community-Led Practices to Build the Worlds We Need* (Cambridge, MA: MIT Press, 2020).

22
Claudia Mareis and Nina Paim, eds., *Design Struggles: Intersecting Histories, Pedagogies, and Perspectives* (Amsterdam: Valiz, 2021), 207.

They asked me to design a house,

reproduced"[24] in both educational and professional fields. Alex Martinis Roe and Fotini Lazaridou-Hatzigoga in *Two Become Two, Propositions for Feminist Collective Practice* argue that architecture can be defined as the design of settings for encounter. Our built environment is deeply intertwined with material politics, shaping relational dynamics by creating spaces that frame and direct our movements and activities. "As inhabitants, we have the agency to repurpose spaces in ways unforeseen by their designers."[25] However, these adaptations always involve material negotiations – between permanent features like walls, floors, and ceiling, and the evolving functions of the space. Building on this perspective, we aim to contribute to the discourse on domesticity by emphasizing its dual nature; not only as social space but indeed as a "spatial space."[26] By opening the dialogue on inhabitants' "spatial agency,"[27] we seek to underline its fundamental role in shaping the built environment and its potential to redefine the future of spatial design. Key in this objective is a shift away from the assumption that architects and designers are the only ones able to intervene in such a discourse. Instead, we aim to destabilize and decenter certain historiographical presumptions, for example, by attributing architectural authorship to non-expert individuals, who "may have lacked signature, but not significance."[28]

In pursuit of a spatial discourse on the complexities of the domestic environment, and in pursuit of a different approach to knowledge, one that, as Luce Beeckams proposes, "is more consistently informed by the affections and complexity of human lived experience,"[29] we position ourselves as curators and moderators of this discussion throughout this book.
Our research journey began when we chose to collaborate – as women, as close friends, and as individuals rooted in struggles to introduce alternative frameworks for the design process of domestic environments within the architectural field, both inside and outside academia. Along the way, we encountered, discovered, and engaged with the perspectives of many others working in this space. For us, conversations and shared experiences are fundamental starting points to challenge the dominant narratives that shape the design of domestic environments.
We align with Luce Beeckmans, Alessandra Gola, Ashika Singh in recognizing that our role as curators and moderators of this discussion is shaped by historical contexts in which women have

23 Harriet Harriss and Emily Eliza Scott, "What Forms Might Feminist Pedagogy Take in Architecture and Who Are Its Potential Protagonists (Imaginary or Real)?," *Making Trouble to Stay With: Architecture and Feminist Pedagogies, no. 1 (2017): 92.*

24 Torsten Lange et al., "Making Trouble to Stay With: Architecture and Feminist Pedagogies," *Field 7,* no. 1 (November 2017): 90.

25 Alex Martinis Roe, *To Become Two - Propositions for Feminist Collective Practice* (Berlin: Archive Books, 2018), 178.

26 Beeckmans et al., *Making Home(s) in Displacement,* 15.

27 Nishat Awan, Tatjana Schneider, and Jeremy Till, *Spatial Agency: Other Ways of Doing Architecture* (London and New York: Routledge, 2013).

28 Anooradha Iyer Siddiqi and Rachel Lee, "On Margins: Feminist Architectural Histories of Migration," *ABE Journal. Architecture beyond Europe,* no. 16 (December 31, 2019).

29 Beeckmans et al., *Making Home(s) in Displacement,* 25.

long been designated as homemakers. This includes an awareness of housework, class, racialization, gender, and the dynamic between private and public spaces,[30] which inevitably frames this publication. At the same time, we acknowledge our relatively privileged position – as white, cis, able-bodied women – in exploring these themes, enabling us to contribute to the debate intentionally and "on our own terms."[31]

This book is divided into two sections. The first one, *Reflections,* is a collection of stories, histories, dialogues, anecdotes, reflections, imaginings, and hopes regarding domestic life. This collection is varied in terms of geography, discipline, and format, aiming to offer an engaging and multifaceted entry point[32] for reconsidering the spatial approach to domesticity. We carried out an informal way of doing research, along with more formal research methods like interviews[33] that we address here as "conversations." Acknowledging their limitations in accuracy we highlight their openness and ability to bring layers of thought and imagination to the reader. Through this collection, we hope to connect with many other lived experiences and at the same time to contribute to a practice of archiving knowledge that is based on relational structures.
Homes are seen here as foundational spaces that allow different complexities and subjectivities to manifest with care. However, the design of homes often overlooks the care required to foster such diversity, as it falls outside the principles most commonly prioritized by the discipline of architecture, particularly domestic architecture. How, then, can we reimagine or repurpose the interior space "in ways that open up a wide range of possibilities for sustaining and practicing the kinds of relationships that will support us across the life course?"[34]

The first section of this book draws attention to these overlooked aspects, proposing a set of alternative principles to guide the design of domestic spaces. It emphasizes the role of architecture, considering how the interior evolved beyond its constructional, ornamental and surface definition, to become an architectural concept.[35] Rather than viewing architecture solely as a board discipline, we approach it as a relational practice – one that activates the process of reimagining and creating spaces where things can "unfold otherwise."[36] By reframing the design of homes through this perspective, we aim to prioritize care, diversity, and the evolving needs of inhabitants as central to the practice of domestic architecture.

They asked me to design a house,

30
Ibid, 26

31
Ibid.

32
Huda Tayob and Suzanne Hall, *Race, Space and Architecture: Towards an Open-Access Curriculum* (London, UK: London School of Economics and Political Science, Department of Sociology, 2019), 3.

33
Martinis Roe, *To Become Two,* 16.

34
Leslie Kern, *Feminist City: Claiming Space in a Man-Made World* (London and New York: Verso Books, 2020), 81.

35
Charles Rice, *The Emergence of the Interior: Architecture, Modernity, Domesticity* (Abingdon: Routledge, 2007), 3.

36
Kern, *Feminist City,* 57.

The second section, *Exercises,* explores ways to put these ideas into action. Through a series of narrative texts, we share insights to navigate the complexities of domestic space, whether as designers or dwellers. Workshops are central to our approach, serving as a form of (design) resistance. In these settings, we spontaneously began using collective drawing to promote a communication that could be other than verbal, that could set the individuals more free in expressing and sharing their stories. We soon realized the power of imagination that a drawing practice can bring, and started to be enriched by so many new, different perspectives regarding the domestic environment. We noticed how collective drawing fostered connections during workshops, becoming a catalyst for dialogue and shared understanding. It soon became a cornerstone of our approach, helping to shape how we think about and address domestic spaces.

Phyllis Birkby initiated the "Women's Environmental Fantasies" project in 1973, where she encouraged women to draw their fantasy environments. Through these workshops, women could reimagine domestic and communal spaces, fostering a sense of empowerment and ownership over their environments.[37] Inspired by Birkby's work, we recognize the transformative potential of drawing as a tool for reimagining domestic life. This section is an open diary of our experiences with collective drawing, carried out in different workshop sessions. Much like Birkby's workshops, we aim to offer a space for reclaiming and redefining environments, encouraging a more inclusive and diverse approach to design.
It was equally important for us to extend this space into the pages of this publication. To this end, this section includes interactive exercises for readers, inviting them to engage with the propositions, discoveries, and reflections shared throughout the publication. In a way, this section is designed for anyone inspired to explore and test their own insights as they navigate these pages.

37 Birkby, "Making Room," 28–29.

Ilaria and Georgina asked them to design a home

Inherently tied to space. Closely connected to the decorative. A reminder of the presence of hospitality. A shared exercise in practicing domesticity.

They asked me to design a house,

Part one
Reflections

From the Balcony

Lara Schrijver
Noemi Biasetton and Valentina Rizzi
Platon Issaias
Feven Gebeyehu Zeru
Panos Dragonas
Ines Glowania
Edit Collective

INTRODUCTION

The contemporary understanding of dwelling is marked by a fundamental rethinking of boundaries: between home and city, private and public life, formal and informal modes of inhabitation – as well as modes of design spaces – and inherited traditions and emerging forms of living. This shift reflects how domestic life is shaped not only by architectural form, but by broader social, economic, and cultural transformations.

Beyond its material manifestations, the home carries affective, symbolic, and political significance. It mediates relationships between bodies, communities, and territories, shaping how we inhabit both private spaces and shared environments. As societies evolve through migration, technological change, and shifting social bonds, the very notion of dwelling transforms, challenging inherited frameworks and calling for new spatial and conceptual approaches to domestic life. This chapter brings together voices from diverse geographies and histories, exploring how the domestic realm intersects with urban, political, and ecological dimensions.

Our conversation with Lara Schrijver traces the shifting role of architecture in shaping social relations, questioning how domestic space operates as both a site of care and a political arena. Noemi Biasetton and Valentina Rizzi examine the contested realities of dwelling in Venice, a city suspended between romantic decay and aggressive tourist commodification. Through activist and artistic practices, they propose collective forms of intimacy - beyond the private home - that address the city's social and ecological tensions.

Feven Gebeyehu Zeru's study of Addis Ababa brings into view the entanglement of formal and informal urban practices, revealing how residents creatively adapt and negotiate these overlapping systems to sustain social life and urban cohesion. In Athens, Panos Dragonas investigates the adaptability of the *polykatoikia* – a traditional multi-family residential building – to new forms of living,

They asked me to design a house,

showing how this architectural typology embodies layered histories of both social integration and exclusion.

Ines Glowania's reflections show how the hybrid homes of the digital age unsettle long-standing architectural ideas of fixity, scale, and function, as the home stretches beyond its walls to become a platform for rethinking work, care, and belonging. Platon Issaias emphasizes the inherently political nature of architecture, analyzing how domestic spaces both reflect and reproduce social inequalities, especially within contexts marked by economic instability and migration.

The conversation with Edit Collective brings these discussions into a feminist and activist register, emphasizing the importance of collaborative, community-driven practices that challenge dominant narratives of domesticity.

This chapter proposes an understanding of the domestic as a space where political agency, cultural memory, and social belonging take form. Whether through feminist critiques of architectural education, reflections on cooperative housing, or calls to rethink standards of comfort and efficiency, the contributors in this chapter challenge us to expand our understanding of domesticity. How might reimagining the domestic realm enable architecture to hold space for care, plurality, and difference? Collectively, these contributions map out ways of dwelling that are adaptable, interconnected, and open to reinvention. They resist fixed definitions and singular narratives, offering instead insights into how the home, in its many forms, becomes a lens for understanding and reimagining the politics, practices, and possibilities of contemporary urban life.

From the balcony,
where everyday gestures

weave

into

collective

life.

Ilaria and Georgina asked them to design a home

They asked me to design a house,

On Architecture, Domesticity, and the Common
Conversation with Lara Schrijver

ILARIA AND GEORGINA We met during Rotterdam Architecture Month at the presentation of the book *Women in Architecture*, a project you were involved in. Could you tell us about the journey that brought you to that moment?

LARA I've been working in and teaching architecture for a long time, mainly in history and theory. I finished my studies at the end of the 1990s, so really in the "heydays" of neoliberalism, but also in a period of great optimism. The internet still seemed positive, with fewer privacy concerns and less data mining. And when the Berlin wall came down in 1989, there was a sense that things were shifting in Europe. There were a lot of reasons to be optimistic at the time. In my own circles, we were simultaneously aware of feminist issues and worked hard to show our 'equal value' in the workplace. In architecture, there was a lot of interesting experimentation in housing, on what the 'smart home' could be, and speculations on how we could shape some level of common space around the houses. It was a very different period when some tough topics, like the 'other' voice of the feminine, were simply not discussed. Of course these topics might pop up occasionally – I remember in particular Francesca Hughes presenting her book on women architects at the *ANYhow* conference in Rotterdam in 1997. In retrospect, I have a lot of questions about the 1990s, because the freedom and optimism we felt at the time did not pay off – the 20 years that followed were in many ways devastating. The current housing crisis is related not only to a lack of sufficient living space but also to the fact that some people are profiting from it, while others are unable to find even basic accommodation. Urgencies like the housing crisis seem to be coming together into a question of how to raise voices of care and how to work towards a society that adequately cares for everyone and not just for a few. In retrospect, these concerns may have continued to develop in feminist and postcolonial thinking, but were less in the spotlight in the 1990s. For the past five years, this has led me to look more specifically into the disciplinary habits and mechanisms within my own teaching. I think about how we can initiate conversations that haven't been opened up before; particularly regarding how urban planning, architecture, and design structures contribute to processes of injustice. I discuss these questions with colleagues and students, to address these very deep-seated structures that are often unjust, asymmetrical, unfair, and that contribute to systemic exclusions. That's what led me to that afternoon on feminist architecture practices where we met. I guess I'm just looking for a way to help these upcoming generations that give voice to a lot of these things.

ILARIA How can the correlation between domesticity and the social context be introduced in educational environments?

LARA This is a big question. In my teaching, I focus on revealing connections. Our societal values structure the way we build, while what we build can also push back at these values, or be reconfigured as society evolves. I talk to my students about disciplinary autonomy on one side, and societal service on the other side. It's very unusual for architects to build with their own money; in this sense, you're a service industry, trying to adapt to social needs yet also complicit with vested interests. On the other hand, there's a very distinct disciplinary autonomy, formed through practice and in conversation with colleagues, that can set a new agenda – which is also what you're doing here – and that can help to rethink commonalities. Architecture is somewhere in between, going back and forth between autonomy and service.

Today, movements like cohousing, cooperative housing, and other alternative ways of financing and organizing how we live in smaller communities are gaining momentum. This signals a kind of pushback from within the discipline itself, offering responses to the inefficiencies of highly individualized housing models. At the same time, it echoes long-standing themes in feminist thought, giving the sense that we're treading familiar ground – underscoring a recurring amnesia when it comes to recent histories. For example, in the book *The Grand Domestic Revolution. A History of Feminist Designs for American Homes, Neighborhoods and Cities* Dolores Hayden discusses a 1915 (!) proposal for kitchenless houses by Alice Constance Austin. This was meant to reduce housework and make shared household tasks a collective endeavor.

GEORGINA ❦ What you say reminds me of the book *The Minimum Dwelling* by Karel Teige, where he states that the minimum dwelling in a collective house must be conceived as an individual living cell, with a bedroom but without the kitchen or further facilities; or that these facilities should be available as collective services. The pattern of family life would be broken and each individual could be free from this burden in order to exploit their potential for participation in public life.

LARA ❦ The Soviet Constructivists were perhaps the most radical in removing the kitchen and making collective units. When kitchen and laundry facilities, along with all these domestic elements, are shared and distributed, they place less burden on individual families.

Unfortunately in current high-rise buildings the communal space has often become incredibly small. This leaves little opportunity for shared facilities and interaction outside the home, which in a way is really sad because much of the value in architecture has been about finding social fabrics and spaces to interact outside of the home.

When you view housing as offering profits rather than living space, your focus shifts to maximizing the square meters that someone will pay for in your floor plan, rather than prioritizing the maximum experience necessary for fostering connections.

ILARIA ❦ Talking about housing as a profit mechanism rather than looking at the experiences of a living space makes me think about the long-discussed, also philosophical, dualism between home and house.

LARA ❦ It's true that making a 'home' has traditionally been viewed as part of the

They asked me to design a house,

feminine domain. That connects to an essay I once wrote about Disney princesses and the kinds of domestic spaces they inhabit. What do Snow White, Cinderella, and Sleeping Beauty – characters from the 1930s – tell us about women and domestic roles compared to more recent figures like Moana or Mulan? Interestingly, the early princesses are closely tied to the kitchen – their safe spaces are deeply domestic. This can certainly be read as restrictive, but it becomes more nuanced when we consider Hannah Arendt's distinction between the public and private realms. She suggests that the social and familial spheres serve as training grounds for how we eventually participate in society – offering a different lens on these domestic roles. If we consider the home as the place where children learn, experiment, and begin to shape their relationships, then it becomes a crucial building block for how we engage with the outside world. Sometimes, when we discuss Arendt's feminist principles, we tend to overlook what she said about private space. There's often a strong emphasis on the importance of public spaces – but when we reflect on how our relationship to home shapes the way we participate in the public sphere, it becomes even more vital to examine the home with care. I wouldn't go so far as to claim that architectural discourse in recent years has clearly shifted from house to home – or from housing to home to house – but that would certainly make for an interesting study.

GEORGINA ⚱ Exactly – the domestic environment is complex. It can be explored from anthropological, social, or psychological perspectives. Perhaps due to our background, we tend to see it first and foremost as a space. And if we accept that space can influence behavior patterns over time, then what role does education – starting from the university years – play in shaping and constructing domesticities?

LARA ⚱ When you talk about *shaping space*, you're already approaching it from an architectural perspective. But education can – and should – broaden that discussion to include how we *shape relationships*, and how the home influences our future ways of seeing and engaging with the world. Over the past five years, there's been growing awareness of distinct cultural narratives. We're now starting to explore how these varied *shapes* and *relations* can be interpreted through different lenses. Just recently – in September 2023 – *Germane Barnes* gave a lecture at the *Nieuwe Instituut* in Rotterdam, reflecting on *Black identity* and *domesticity.* He explored how *domestic space* relates to *public space*, focusing on the porch as a typology rooted in African traditions, shaped through the American context, and gradually formalized. The *porch*, as he described it, is that threshold space – where you sit outside your house, facing the public realm. For him, it represented a kind of safe space, but one with a limit. Beyond the porch was the *public space* – a space where, as a young Black man in the U.S., he became visible and vulnerable to being targeted, attacked, or arrested.
I grew up in the northeastern U.S., and I recognize the kind of *porch* space he described. But I never experienced that spatial threshold as a boundary of safety.

Lara asked them to design a home

As a young white suburban kid, the porch felt more fluid – *public space* didn't carry the same threat. That contrast in lived experience reveals how domestic and public spaces are not neutral – and how *architecture* intersects with *identity*. These differences open space for new conversations – ones that are informed by *architecture*, but grounded in diverse, specific realities.

ILARIA ⚲ Thinking about boundaries between the public and the private, I think we should talk about places that are not private or public, but common. Do you address this in your work too?

LARA ⚲ I am glad that you raise this question. In the 1990s, collective space was a hot topic, with scholars and practitioners questioning the public-private binary. In my own research I was particularly interested in how Venturi and Brown talked about private spaces, public spaces, and civic spaces in *Learning from Las Vegas*. Civic spaces are where we engage with each other on a polite and societal level. I like the civic alongside the communal or the collective because the civic assumes a kind of appropriate behavior to engage with one another. In civic space, you deal with the better appeals of society and not only with your own desire. For me, there is also a difference between the civic and the collective because the latter assumes a kind of voluntary membership. Whereas in civic space, there is a level of mutual engagement that you need to allow for the presence of others. We don't have to get along or be friendly with everyone, but the question is whether we can adequately interact and have the space for those who want to get along.

ILARIA ⚲ Is architecture the discipline that can facilitate these relations to happen in an inclusive way?

LARA ⚲ Again this is a complicated question: I would tend to say yes, but it also comes down to how it is shaped, how it materializes, and how it is formed. And then, when you replicate models that lack extra spaces beyond the bare minimum for existence, you are taking away much of the richness of spatial territories. This is one of the problems we are running into with a universalist discourse. For this, I think Quill R. Kukla's book *City Living* is a wonderful, legible reflection on the city, its territorialities and its inhabitants. The argument is that if you take a step back and look at the city, what you want from it is to allow for many and multiple territorialities. The risk of the universalist discourse is that you make it flat, too simple. The author says that there are certain territorialities that suit some people, while others are meant for other people. This means they don't feel comfortable and appropriate in each and every one of them, but they have access to spaces that work for them; while a universalist approach suggests that *all* of the city should be comfortable to *everyone*. This way, we can begin to think about how these things tie together, how the domestic can become the training ground, a personal space that is adequate to the self, but also serves to learn appropriate and polite interactions with others. To me,

They asked me to design a house,

this mode of approaching the world can be situated in the domestic, in the home, but in a broader way than the traditional nuclear family. bell hooks, whose work is important to this line of thinking, discusses kinship and family much more than blood relations. These ties are formed in the house but spread out to inform society. While the last 20 years have been marked by many struggles, we're also gaining new and interesting perspectives because there's simply more room to talk about them.

GEORGINA ✎ I want to share something that is related to my experience here in The Netherlands, where all the houses are built the same. The same doors, the same windows, the same amount of rooms. I don't know if you are familiar with the phenomenon of *Polikatoikia* (apartment building) in Athens. All buildings are built the same, as well. How can we finally shape subjectivities, if we continue to have massive architecture planning? How do we create intimate spaces?

LARA ✎ That's a huge question. For me, it involves numerous intertwined threads of thinking. In the book *Four Walls and a Roof*, Reinier de Graaf expresses his concerns about viewing housing as a profit model. When you describe buildings with the same layout and windows, I think of buildings where people can 'drift through', which makes me think of migrants, expats, temporary laborers. These spaces are meant to remain untouched or not to 'stick' in your mind but rather provide basic amenities. Earlier, you talked about shaping these domestic spaces, and I think we might want to return to a more participatory/DIY approach, to a mode where architecture sets conditions, but we don't assume they always stay that way. For example, the work of Teddy Cruz and Fonna Forman stands out for their ability to shape the internal workings of a town, but without a preconceived idea of how the town functions, or should function. Their approach involves deep participatory actions, engaging with people to uncover habits and gathering spaces, and emphasizing collaborative engagement. It challenges the modernist illusion of having a universal answer for everyone, and focuses on their expertise in shaping space based on the needs of the community. Looking back at self-build communities in North America, or what the Matrix collective did in their close collaboration with communities in London, or the social housing project Malieklos that was awarded the 2022 Rotterdam Architecture Prize, these serve as examples of people who invested *time* and *care* into their projects. My concern is that we live in a profit-oriented, efficiency-structured society, where many of these creative projects, done with time and love, seem not to fit.

ILARIA ✎ At the beginning of our conversation, you said that you are trying to help younger generations navigate through these hard times and create a better future.

GEORGINA ✎ Yes, it gives hope to our generation, talking to you and seeing that you want to talk to us. A hope that we really need.

Lara asked them to design a home

LARA ⚱ Thank you. And alongside hope, we need some humility. Architecture can't fix the world, but it can help. And maybe it can also let go of this artificial division between domestic space and urban planning, because even tiny initiatives can spread.

ILARIA ⚱ Step by step.

They asked me to design a house,

Lara asked them to design a home

LARA SCHRIJVER is professor in architecture theory at the University of Antwerp. Her research focuses on twentieth-century architecture and its theories. She is author of *Oswald Mathias Ungers and Rem Koolhaas* (2021) and editor of *The Tacit Dimension: Architecture Knowledge and Scientific Research* (2021).
She is co-editor of *Autonomous Architecture in Flanders* (2016) and *Women in Architecture* (2023), and has served as editor for the *KNOB Bulletin, Footprint* journal and *OASE.*

They asked me to design a house,

A Pinch of Rust, a Dash of Mistrust… …and a Little Bit of Pixie Dust: Overcoming Utopias in Venice

Noemi Biasetton and Valentina Rizzi

Venice is often perceived as a quirky blend of a fairytale and a sinking Atlantis – charming, yet slightly on the verge of falling apart. From the early twentieth century, the narrative surrounding Venice has been intrinsically linked to the idea of its death. From Thomas Mann's renowned novella *Death in Venice*[38] to Settis's book *If Venice Dies*,[39] the islands of the lagoon seem to harbor within them a source of romantic sadness that makes the city an inexorable source of distress and confrontation with its past – making it impossible to redirect its future. Similarly, in the less romanticized and more down-to-earth narrative, hordes of tourists travel daily to this anomalous city in order to catch one last glimpse of a territory that – supposedly – may no longer exist in a few decades. A narrative that, as we well know, has definitely proved prolific for the pockets of those in the city who have turned tourism into their source of profit.

Despite its challenges, Venice continues to harbor small pockets of resistance – citizen committees, university associations, and activist collectives – who, for several years, have been striving to bring local and international attention to the city's ongoing issues. In fact, especially in the post-Covid years, the debate about the city has been powerfully rekindled focusing – among other things[40] – on the issue of the city's depopulation, the phenomenon of overtourism,[41] and the impossible economic standards dictated by the real estate market. Unfortunately, in Italy, the broader issue of residency remains largely overlooked, often engulfed by speculation about sustainability, phantom projects to increase the population, and the privatization of the city with entrance tickets and fees. Most of the time these deeds are considered futile by many observers, including the mayor of Venice himself, who stare in disbelief at the waste of effort to "actually" live in a place that apparently deserves no redemption. Hiding behind the image of a terminally ill patient, attempting a real cure is no longer an option.

38
Thomas Mann, *Death in Venice* (New York: Knopf, 1965).

39
Salvatore Settis, *If Venice Dies* (New York: New Vessel Press, 2016).

40
There are numerous collectives and advocacy projects in the Venice area, including the independent space network ComeCome, and initiatives like BUrb (Biennale Urbana), which critically engage with the Biennale system. Other notable groups include Comitato No Grandi Navi (opposing cruise ships in the lagoon), housing and lagoon preservation organizations such as ASC, Ocio, and PovegliaPerTutti, as well as committees dedicated to public health protection and enhancement, alongside various neighborhood associations.

41
Giacomo-Maria Salerno and Antonio Paolo Russo, 'Venice as a Short-Term City. Between Global Trends and Local Lock-Ins', *Journal of Sustainable Tourism* 30, no. 5 (4 May 2022): 1040–59.

Noemi and Valentina asked them to design a home

Figure 1
Graphics for citizens demonstration. Francesco Bevilacqua, 2024. Courtesy of the author.

Figure 2
Evil Brugnaro. Stian Rampoldi, 2024. Courtesy of the author.

They asked me to design a house,

Those who live in Venice know that the city is certainly sick, but not (yet) dying. Venice is dust, brick, water, fog, moisture, mudflats, mould, bridges, boundaries. Venice is also progressive reduction of public healthcare, inadequate public transportation, skyrocketing tourist pressure, lack of preschools, disappearance of local shops, vacant apartments in public housing. The touristic routes of the city and its narrow alleys help to conceal these conflicting faces – one of allure, the other of deception. Behind its polished façades, the governance can hide their blatant disregard for the city, skillfully hiding the cracks beneath a dazzling exterior.

Even after only a few months in the city, each new citizen realizes quite independently that the establishment of care systems is as essential to their own survival as that of their domestic environment. The dweller and the city environment become symbionts: one cannot exist without the other. Host and guest become a breathing membrane employed in a system of mutual aid that determines one's own death or survival. This symbiont exists in various scalar forms, one ringed in the other: the inhabitant and the room, the room and the house, the house and the *sestiere,*[42] the sestiere and the island, the island and the lagoon, and so on. From the domestic realm, forms of socio-ecological intimacy can propagate into the city, pouring into it a value system related to symbiotic collaborations within the urban.
But how can we activate this chemistry amidst the constant frictions that animate the public debate in Venice? And how can situated projects embody discourses of intimacy within artistic and design practices in the territory of the lagoon?

42 *Sestiere* indicates one of the six zones into which the city of Venice is divided.

In the last five years, we have witnessed a renewed contemporary interest in spatialities defined at the "margin," which often unfold and/or arise as a penetration into pseudo-idyllic contexts, far from the uncomfortable and troublesome contradictions of the urban. However, the attention paid to these places for artistic production often runs the risk of succumbing to the allure of the remote hamlet or village, while avoiding confrontation with complex human contexts which, precisely because of their intricacy, require a continuous and concerted action. Such operations always require a processuality capable of being generative beyond the time frame of an external intervention in the circumstance, be it in the city or outside of it. Moving in the direction of urban regeneration

Noemi and Valentina asked them to design a home

necessarily implies working with the Adversarial[43] in order to attempt a generative recovery of instances, places, and ways of making community.

43
Carl Disalvo, *Adversarial Design* (Cambridge, MA: MIT Press, 2012).

44
Tomás Maldonado, *La speranza progettuale. Ambiente e società* (Milan: Feltrinelli, 2022), p. 40.

From this perspective, it is clear that Venice does not admit any form of utopia. Venice is not the tale of a floating miracle. To operate in Venice entails implicating oneself in an urban substrate that is fundamentally condemned and yet accustomed to contamination. Think, for example, of the role that the city's touristification has on habitability. In a sociopolitical context in which access to housing is one of the primary obstacles to the broader right to inhabit and, consequently, to citizenship, the discourse on tourism cannot be dissociated from a broader debate with respect to a contaminated co-existence.
Besides the so-called tourist invasion, one must shed light on the co-existence of local associations, activists, and artistic research movements that raise collective and shared claims aimed at creating new processes of cohabitation within the lagoon.

In this sense, the co-presence in Venice of this multiplicity of bodies and subjectivities can be read as what Argentinian designer and artist Tomás Maldonado defines as the "human environment,"[44] a mediating membrane of the relations of mutual correspondence between reality and the human. This substratum of relations within which bodies enter and follow one another is a response to the human need for a tangible projection of this layering of existential portals of bodies and space. Thus, we cannot and should not escape the inevitable environmental connotation of the human, but rather land on a temporality that promotes, beyond the presence of one's own body, possibilities for the presence of other bodies. This allows us to generatively inhabit the human environment, composed of relationships, bodies, and artifacts while dialoguing with architectural limits. Recognizing ourselves as humans, and then citizens, can lead to an awareness of a processual co-construction with the environment, built space, and the other. Hence the urge to exercise cohabitation as the resistance of citizen bodies implicated in an ongoing codependency with the city.
Dismantling utopias in Venice questions the power dynamics related, on the one hand, to cohabitating with the exogenous factors manifested daily in city dynamics, and on the other hand, to confronting the impossibility of intervening in the architectural

They asked me to design a house,

conformation of the city. Moreover, existing and acting within an environment so profoundly shaped by its spatial and historical institutionalisation, inevitably leads to the reinforcement of attitudes centred on preserving what is already in place. These choices, which limit the imaginative exploration of *fantastic* or *monstrous* alternatives,[45] fix the engagement within Venetian contexts to what is familiar and established.

The effort starts from the identification of processual and participated paths of operationality. Finding alternatives within the territory, through informal confrontations and advocacy initiatives, must be guided by the aim of declining the potential of intimacy beyond the home itself. An expanded approach to the *domestic* attitudes of care offers an opportunity to renegotiate the conditions of habitability and crossing of built space through alliances. In this sense, it is necessary to compromise oneself in order to protect the chance of co-creating futurable citizenry alliances. And perhaps, allow some generative (or disobedient) fairytales to unfold.

45 The terms "fantastic" and "monstrous" are rooted, on one hand, in contemporary art theory concerning radical institutions, and on the other, in the realm of contemporary visual culture and in the debate around art institutions, where the monstrous category is reimagined as a generative approach to embodied practices (see f.e. Sarah Vanhee, 2018; Ilenia Caleo, 2021).

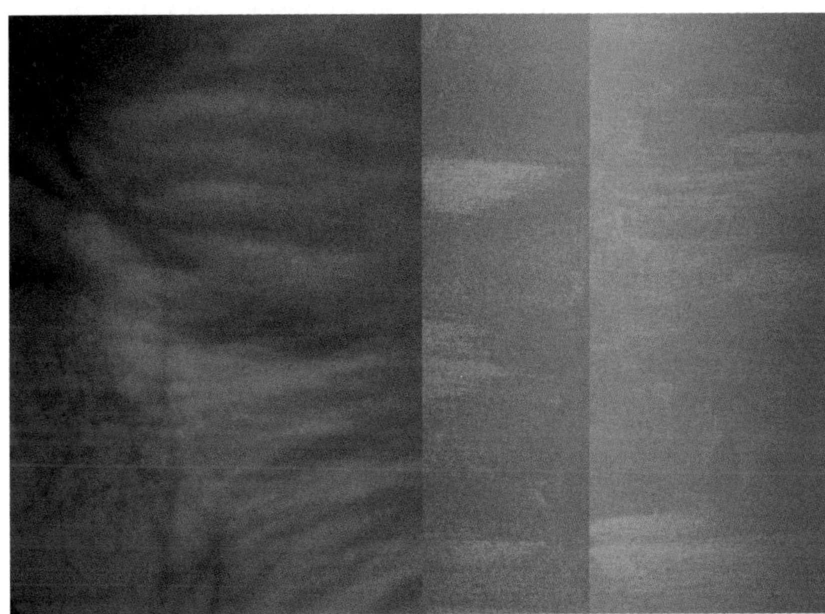

Figure 3
Depositi. Valentina Rizzi, 2021. Courtesy of the author.

NOEMI BIASETTON is a design researcher, writer and editor based in Venice. Her academic studies focus on design cultures and visual representation, with a specific interest in how these are deployed within the social and political dimension. Her practice includes the production of essays and articles, the organization of talks and lectures, and the contribution to research projects for cultural and educational institutions. She is the author of *SUPERSTORM. Design and Politics in the Age of Information* (Onomatopee, 2024).

VALENTINA RIZZI is a researcher and practitioner operating at the intersection of publishing, curating, and critical spatial politics. As a PhD candidate in Visual Arts at Iuav University of Venice, her research delves into visual culture, with a particular emphasis on dwelling and spatial related practices as transformative frameworks for advocacy within the visual arts. She is part of ESPACIAR, an international research group established by the University of Valladolid, and member of OCIO, a grassroots observatory focused on housing rights and residency in Venice.

They asked me to design a house,

Housing and the City: From Regulation to Resistance

Conversation with Platon Issaias

ILARIA AND GEORGINA Can you tell us something about your practice as an architect and educator?

PLATON Since 2009, my work has been shaped by collective collaboration, particularly during the PhD program *The City as a Project,* a research collective set by Pier Vittorio Aureli at the Berlage Institute in 2009. After studying architecture in Thessaloniki, I pursued a postgraduate master's degree at Columbia University in New York, where I met Pier Vittorio. His mentorship and the intellectual connections and friendships with Hamed Khosravi, Maria Shéhérazade Giudici, Francesco Marullo, Amor Djalali, Bernardina Borra, Chris Lee, among others, were instrumental. Together we aimed to rethink the relationship between architecture and the city, not treating them as separate entities. Over the past fifteen years, our collaborative work has evolved, leading to publications and teaching, primarily within the framework of Diploma Unit 7 and the Projective Cities programme, which we co-direct with my closest friend and collaborator, Hamed Khosravi. One could argue that the topics we were exploring in 2008-2009 were quite marginal, but they have become much more common in architectural discourse today.

ILARIA How do you find your case studies? And how did you transition these places from being marginal to being less marginal?

PLATON In the early 2000s, we lived in the euphoria of neoliberal architecture. There was almost no critical discourse, especially from within the architectural field. While scholars in geography, sociology, philosophy, and political theory critiqued late capitalism, architects largely refrained from engaging with these debates. For us, references to radical leftist politics and the Italian autonomist workers' movements, shaped by events like Genoa 2001 and the anti-capitalist movement, were central. Yet, this perspective was missing in architecture. Today a shift is evident, particularly among younger generations, who emphasize an operative approach to history, theory, and critical practice. By examining specific examples within the broader historical context, we uncover marginalized elements left out of the traditional canon. For example, before and along the preparation for the Olympic Games in Athens, there were significant exhibitions of Greek architecture. Athens was central to a discourse about the modern contemporary European city. This view was influenced by celebratory narratives and political positions emphasizing multifunctionality and hybridity – all trends echoed from the European North, very popular in the Netherlands among others. Athens was perceived as the epitome of a type of "peripheral modernity". Recently, Athens has been touted as "the new Berlin", but one wonders if it ever took that direction, or even, what does this phrase means. I looked into the city's evolution from the 1940s until the 2010s. The connection between Greece's economic development, the economic crisis, and the building sector is evident. Other case studies, such as my friend Hamed Khosravi's exploration of

Platon asked them to design a home

the Iranian city, reveal how cosmological and theological ideas, as well as the idea of enclosure, shape city design and architecture, offering reinterpretations of historical narratives.
In our teaching we often emphasize the importance of focusing on specific examples, which can sometimes frustrate students who express a desire to tackle broad topics like the climate crisis or capitalism. However, addressing such expansive themes directly is impractical. Instead, we encourage exploring concrete cases. This approach underscores a fundamental principle shared across all sciences: broader insights must emerge from meticulous, case-based research.

ILARIA ⚘ Based on your perspective, it seems that your work revealed the necessity of interdisciplinarity to foster critical thinking within architecture. Would you agree?

PLATON ⚘ Interdisciplinarity involves incorporating feedback and collaborating with other disciplines. The goal is to produce outcomes that are visible, actionable, and valuable for critical discourse and diverse practices. We have to be careful when we talk about interdisciplinarity because it is also a concept that has been very much mobilized against critical discourse. It has been used to neutralize and present issues as managerial problems. When I speak of interdisciplinarity, I emphasize placing discourse within a broader context and addressing it though a larger, more complex framework.

ILARIA ⚘ You worked on the relationship between policy-making and architectural planning. Could you guide us through this practice?

PLATON ⚘ In my personal research and my work as an educator, I focus on the legal frameworks that shape cities, particularly the regulations governing urbanization and the formation of architectural types. I aim to uncover the political dimensions within architecture's legal context, exploring how it intersects with broader societal issues. This approach unveils multiscalar challenges, from safety and structural stability, to form and heritage preservation. These seemingly apolitical parameters are, in fact, deeply political, influencing labor, economy, and industry interests. Examining regulations, especially during economic crises, reveals how their interpretations often serve specific interests. Through ourpractice Fatura Collaborative, a collective currently formed by Alexandra Vougia, Theodossis Issaias, Giannantonis Moutsatsos, and Myrto Vravosinou, we actively engage with and challenge these regulations, recognizing how even minor details influence building design and, ultimately, our living environments.

GEORGINA ⚘ How do we go from macro to micro? How do these parameters and politics from the outside go into domesticity?

PLATON ⚘ There is a project we worked on for six or seven years that started as a consultancy with the Vietnamese community in Boston. Initially focused on

They asked me to design a house,

designing a day-care center, it evolved into a complex urban design project in Da-Nang, the fifth largest city in Vietnam. We collaborated with groups and collectives from the city to develop four small domestic types within blocks eligible for World Bank-subsidized equal share loans. By rethinking the party wall, we secured building permissions for these units, fostering neighborhood growth. This system, a defense against speculation, connected infrastructure to support vulnerable workers. In Da Nang, the challenge was that special economic zones left precarious agricultural and migrant workers without housing. Our project introduced a collaborative system, addressing both individual and collective needs.

To address your question about how domesticity and the city function, we can reflect on Pierre Patte's 17th-century section of Parisian houses: we are still operating in this paradigm. The fundamental section of domesticity shapes the city, a space where family structures are supposed to exist and individuals are supposed to be formed.

ILARIA Your work clearly challenges the concept of comfort while bridging the gap between economic factors and the users' needs.

PLATON Earlier, we discussed building regulations as an area where standards can be critically questioned. The notion of comfort, tied to the standardization of the body, is notably patriarchal and hierarchical. Notably, key figures in this logic were connected to fascist and Nazi ideologies. This connection between ideology and male practitioners is far from coincidental.

GEORGINA In our education, we never explored the concept of social design, nor did we engage with terms like inclusivity or feminist approaches. How do you, as an educator, address these frameworks in your teaching?

PLATON While inequality persists globally, there's a growing resistance, especially among younger architects and students. The mobilization of practitioners, particularly young women, advocating for radical feminist discourse, is vital for driving change in architecture education and society at large.

GEORGINA What is your personal experience with the user approach when called upon to communicate, discuss, and ultimately decide on the future of their space?

PLATON That's an excellent question. Navigating societal norms can be challenging. Yet, through thoughtful design and communication we aim to challenge norms, even in small ways. Societal, gender, class norms and standards are sometimes very difficult to fight, but you can do certain things. Even the way you talk about stuff could change the way people think about their own space. Designing around people's needs, even if not initially radical, can evolve into something unexpectedly interesting. For example, in a project we finished recently in Northern Greece, almost without making them aware of it,

Platon asked them to design a home

we deconstructed the way a family of four initially imagined their house. Instead of a typical, hierarchical organisation of domestic programs, we designed a house in separate clusters, with independent entries, with a central, open kitchen, and generous outdoor protected spaces and courtyards. This collaboration on smaller, meaningful projects brings us joy, as we steer away from designing large villas and tourist facilities that could negatively impact the environment.

GEORGINA Do you have a wish towards the evolution of architectural education and practice?

PLATON I don't have a definitive answer, but I can share a case study that reflects my perspective. One of the most remarkable examples of societal, economic, urban, and architectural experimentation in the past decade has been Barcelona. This transformation emerged from grassroots social movements advocating for basic rights. You might be familiar with Cristina Gamboa and Lacol cooperative, Cierto Studio, a pioneering studio led by six women, and the excellent MAIO – each of them showcases how small practices can develop projects that can have a meaningful impact.
For instance, Barcelona's cooperative housing movement, which began with just a few buildings, has since gained global resonance. Similar initiatives in Switzerland challenge the traditional notions of overly-designed public spaces. These efforts demonstrate how targeted strategies and tactical approaches, focused on specific, tangible changes, can ultimately lead to transformative shifts. A particularly inspiring moment came from Barcelona en Comù forming a coalition government. After years of preparation, policy discussions, and refining ideas, these activists and thinkers were ready to implement and test their vision. For me, this is a powerful example of the optimism and potential rooted in deliberate planning and sustained grassroots action.

They asked me to design a house,

Platon asked them to design a home

PLATON ISSAIAS (he/him, Athens, 1984) is an architect, researcher, and educator and is co-founder of Fatura Collaborative. He teaches architecture and urban design at the Aristotle University of Thessaloniki and the Architectural Association.

They asked me to design a house,

A Spatial Dialogue in the Emerging City of Addis Ababa: Bridging the Gaps between Informality and Formality

Feven Gebeyehu Zeru

"Modern" Design and Dichotomous Distinctions

As architects, designers, and professionals from diverse disciplines, we all share a well-defined perception of "modern" design. It encapsulates something contemporary, mirroring the essence of the present day. With "modern," we quickly associate the "formal" or, more expansively, the concept of the "developed." At the same time, concepts such as "traditional," "informal," and "undeveloped" entail everything that is not "modern." This dichotomous distinction becomes especially highlighted within the discourse of international urbanization processes, specifically those in the Southern Hemisphere. Thinking in these types of dichotomies is "strongly related to a dialectical mode of analysis, which has not only been a long-standing, intrinsic part of Western culture and discourse but has also always been an important historical frame of reference to position the West against other geographical entities."[46] The juxtaposition of these polarizing concepts leads to a certain oversimplification of reality, a tendency inherent in human nature,[47] where we often find it more convenient to simplify certain aspects rather than grapple with the nuanced realities that often just lie within the middle ground.

46 Sascha Delz, "Spatial Dialogic", in *Lessons of Informality: Architecture and Urban Planning for Emerging Territories. Concepts from Ethiopia*, ed. Felix Heisel and Bisrat Kifle Woldeyessus (Basel: Birkhäuser, 2016), 191.

47 Harold Brookfield, *Interdependent Development* (London: Methuen, 1975), 53.

However, what happens when both dichotomies materialize within a single space?
How do we, as architects, navigate between such polarized concepts?
What if we encounter environments where both formality and informality intertwine?

Plastic sheets and glazed towers: Addis Ababa

One of many places in the "Global South" that encompasses these contrasting realities – the formal and the informal – is Addis Ababa, capital of Ethiopia. It is a city full of contradictions, where high-rise glazed office buildings emerge into self-constructed market stalls made of corrugated steel and plastic sheets. The problematic nature of this polarizing categorization is particularly evident concerning the housing situation in Addis Ababa. Most of the population resides in what is commonly referred to as sefer, a term that, when interpreted through the lens of Western vocabulary describing underdeveloped areas, corresponds to what we would typically label a traditional "slum." However, these traditional settlements have a long history and are an intrinsic part of the city's urban morphology and, therefore, act as important carriers of the city's heritage. The *sefer* are characterized by the fact that families and people still live in close social, economic, as well as spatial proximity.[48] The built structure in these settlements not only facilitates social interaction and a sense of community, but also allows for interaction with the environment, which is an integral part of the daily routine of Ethiopian dwellers. The permeability of the living space connects the interior with the exterior, creating territories that can be used for daily activities like the preparation of food, social interactions, and the generation of income. As a result of the permeability and flexibility of the dwelling, spaces within the home can be utilized not just for *living*, but also for *working*, making these settlements places where living is not separate from working, but exists within it.[49] The modest height makes it easier for residents to adapt their living spaces and use their homes for income-generating activities, fostering a seamless connection to the street. Furthermore, it empowers the residents to be self-constructors through building, repairing, and maintaining their homes according to their needs and preferences.

48 Dirk Hebel and Elias Yitbarek, "Addis Ababa - Extracting Character From Voids", in *Building Ethiopia*, ed. Zegeye Cherenet and Helawi Sewnet (Addis Ababa: EiABC, 2012), 33.

49 Felix Heisel, "Housing Typologies - A Case Study in Addis Ababa", in *Building Ethiopia*, ed. Zegeye Cherenet and Helawi Sewnet (Addis Ababa: EiABC, 2012), 268.

Formalization of Housing

However, the increase in population and the fast migration from rural to urban areas have made these spaces unsustainable. The government attempted to tackle this problem by formalizing housing through the implementation of the Grand Housing Program (GHP), a project which, in collaboration with the German Technical Cooperation (GTZ), gave birth to the so-called Condominiums. A mass-produced, large-scale housing scheme that not only created a vast amount of housing in a short time but also provided multiple employment possibilities aimed at replacing the sefer. Even if the GHP represents a significant leap forward in addressing housing needs, a closer examination of its exterior and interior structures reveals a departure from traditional living patterns. The design concept seems more aligned with a global, "modern"

They asked me to design a house,

approach to housing rather than drawing from the rich tapestry of former inner-city habitation. In stark contrast to traditional settlements, the Condominium buildings are towering blocks with standardized apartment sizes and lack organic spatial and programmatic connections. Even though each compound has an assigned community building for communal activities, its detached location from the apartment blocks makes its integration into daily life quite difficult. Overall, it seems like the needs of the people are oversimplified to the extent that the architecture of the Condominium could belong to any community across the globe.

Although it is important to note that traditional settlements are no longer sustainable for Addis and that Condominium blocks are generally a positive contribution, this example clearly shows how a dichotomous mindset is harmful to the built environment. Despite the challenges often associated with informal settlements and the stigmatization of being labeled as "slums," they indeed offer profound insights into their residents' daily lives, experiences, and perspectives. These insights are a rich resource that should greatly inform and enrich contemporary housing projects. However, to truly integrate these valuable insights into housing projects, we must first address and dispel the degrading stigma associated with the term "slum." This pejorative label implies an imperative to eradicate, thereby exacerbating the existing dichotomies further. Rather than perpetuating a narrative of demonization versus glorification, we must adopt a more pragmatic view of these realities and focus on "the real city, the real economy, and the real social practices and identities of the majority of urbanites who are building our cities if we want to make sense of them."[50] The consequence of this approach no longer offers a clear picture with contrasts, but a picture full of shades of gradations that are not so easy to categorize.

50 Edgar Pieterse, 'Grasping the Unknowable: Coming to Grips with African Urbanisms', *Social Dynamics* 37, no. 1 (March 2011): 28.

Researching the "formal" and the "informal"

As a German-Ethiopian architectural designer, I see myself at the intersection of both contrasting realities and struggle to define my attitude towards this development. On the one hand, it must be acknowledged that the need for housing is pressing, and such large-scale projects provide a tangible solution to address that need. However, on the other hand, this project seems unable to address the intangible living culture of the people. Intrigued by this internal conflict, I wanted to address this issue through a project of my own. Rather than relying on abstract concepts and artificial boundaries, I entered a spatial dialogue where I aimed to unravel some of the dichotomies by immersing myself in the stories and experiences found on site. My aim was to gain a genuine understanding of the specific spatial needs of Ethiopian dwellers that housing in Ethiopia must fulfill in order to ensure the expression of their culture of everyday life.

For this reason, I embarked on a journey that began in August 2022 and continued from November to December of the same year, where I equipped myself with ethnographic research methods and engaged my family in the process. With their help, I was able to visit a multitude of inner-city settlements and Condominium sites. I met various warm-hearted, welcoming people, entered a multitude of homes, and was able to become part of the residents' daily lives. By analyzing these lived spaces through observations, photography, and sketches, coupled with informal conversations with residents, I gained valuable insights into the local living culture and the diverse ways in which residents navigate their daily lives within their domestic spaces. These insights challenged and expanded my initial assumptions, revealing nuanced and complex relationships between dwellers and their living spaces. Following my research trip, I elaborated on my findings, compiling them in the form of collages and abstracted models. Initially, I started to do that as a way of documenting; however, the model-making process became a method to dismantle my observations. Lacking documentation of the actual floor plans, I reconstructed the homes using photographs, relying on the placement of prominent furniture pieces as a reference to understand the surrounding spaces. Through the combination of photographs and comments, I aimed to create a holistic understanding of the domestic space (fig. 1–2).

Through this method, I was able to juxtapose two completely opposite places and ways of living: a small house in Kirko, one of the poorest settlements in Addis Ababa, and a flat in a Condominium in Yeka Ababa, one of the newest Condominium projects in the periphery. A significant finding of my research was the unexpected similarity in the relationships between the residents and their completely different interior and exterior living spaces. Inside, one is immediately struck by the very similarly furnished living rooms.

They asked me to design a house,

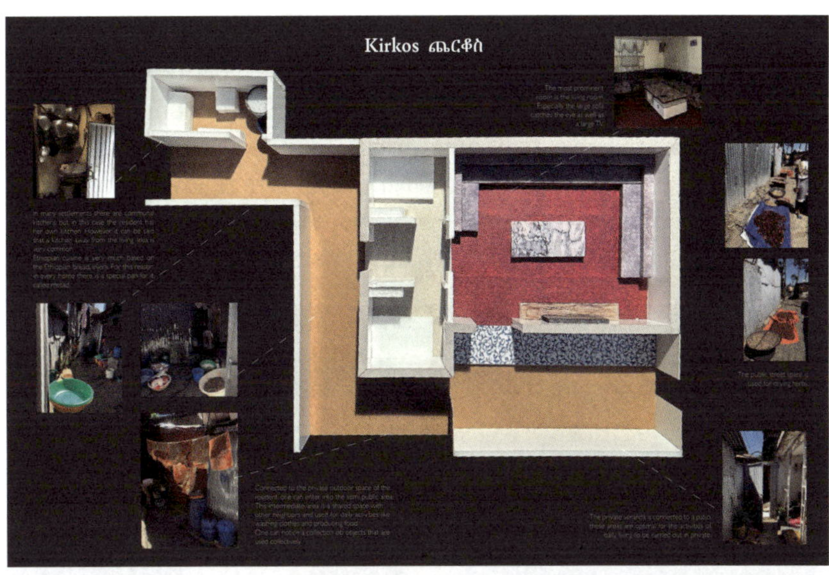

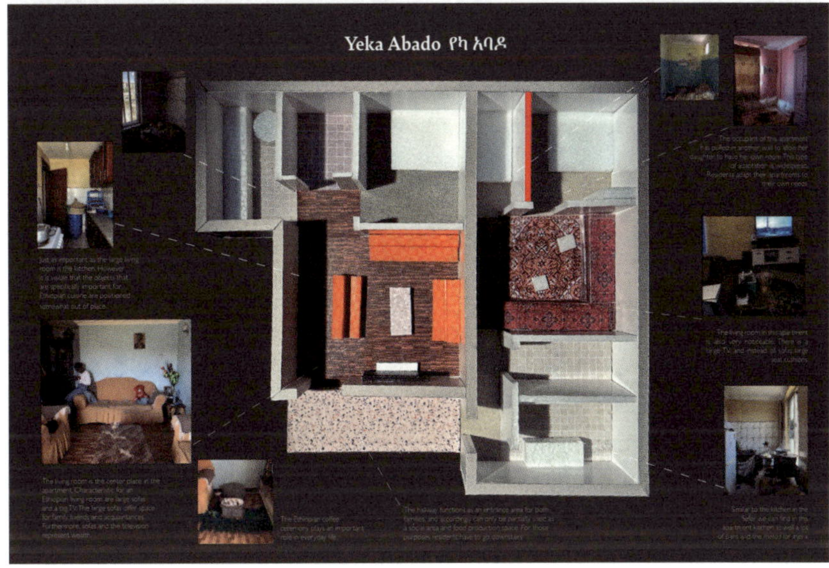

Figure 1 – 2
Floorplan models of a house in Kirkos and apartments in Yeka Abado. Photo-collage, Feven Gebeyehu Zeru, 2023. Source: personal archive. Copyright: Feven Gebeyehu Zeru.

Large sofas, a marble sofa table, and a large television can be seen as the main component of any Ethiopian home. Spaces like the bedrooms, on the other hand, are not given much attention, as most of the daily activities revolve around the living area. Especially in Kirkos, I witnessed a big part of the day happening within the threshold of the home, such as porches, private smaller patios, and communal outdoor corners. In these spaces, hidden from the public realm, daily activities within the community take place, like washing clothes, preparing food, or just daily conversations with the neighbors.

In contrast to the *sefer*, the transitions from private to public in the Condominium are very harsh. The communal corridors are directly connected to the homes, leaving no space for communal activity and all the objects of domesticity found in the communal niches in the *sefer*. However, even within the more rigid structures of Condominiums, I witnessed how residents still appropriated the space by hanging their clothes or placing personal objects (fig. 3).

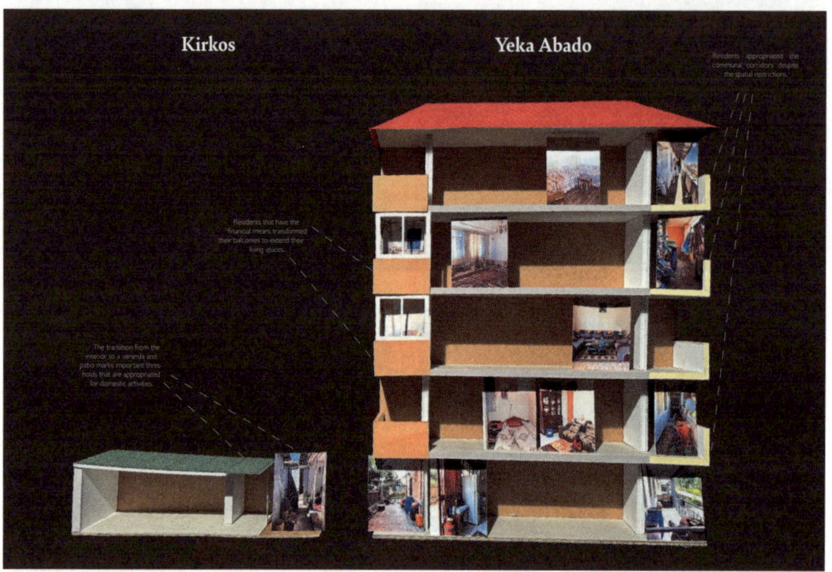

Figure *3*
Section models of a house in Kirkos and apartments in Yeka Abado. Photo-collage, Feven Gebeyehu Zeru, 2023. Source: personal archive. Copyright: Feven Gebeyehu Zeru.

The intertwining of cultural activities with specific spatial conditions became quite evident to me and emphasized the significance of thresholds that offer multiple gradients from private to public spaces. Furthermore, I witnessed how the balcony, often highly desired in German homes, was sometimes completely enclosed and transformed into another room or used to expand the living room or kitchen. Additionally, in many homes, new partitions were added to create extra living space. These interventions highlighted the residents' determination to shape their living spaces according to their needs, overcoming the limitations imposed by the architecture, which made me understand that architecture may set spatial boundaries but cannot dictate how spaces are actually used. I observed that certain cultural practices were affected by the restrictions on cultural expansion within Condominiums, leading residents to abandon or modify certain activities of their everyday lives. For instance, the production of homemade products started to decline with the construction of the Condominiums. The general

They asked me to design a house,

sentiment among the people appears to be marked by conflicting opinions. Residents in the *sefer* express contentment with their current living situation while recognizing the Condominiums as a viable means to generate income, as many Condominium owners opt to rent them out rather than reside in them. On the other hand, those residing in the Condominiums express overall satisfaction with owning a unit but voice concerns about the dearth of community bonding and social cohesion within the Condominium environment.

Bridging the Gaps

During my time in Addis, and as I analyzed my findings, a significant realization dawned on me: the striking closeness between formal and informal housing. Despite the apparent contrast in architectural form and context, people exhibit similar behaviors in appropriating their living spaces. The comparison between informal dwelling houses and formal Condominiums highlighted a crucial insight, particularly within the Ethiopian context: The necessity to design transitional spaces that create gradients from private to public realms, mirroring the setup in the informal settlements. These thresholds have immense potential to serve as areas for residents to personalize and engage in their daily routines. Moreover, observing the way residents interact with their built surroundings underscores their inclination to challenge spatial constraints by adapting balconies and modifying walls. These actions highlight the need for flexible floorplan configurations that allow residents to easily appropriate and adapt their living spaces to align with their needs and preferences.

The presence of traditional practices within *formal* housing emphasizes the blurred boundaries between these conventional categories. In reality, the way people interact with their living spaces is a unique blend of both concepts, rendering the strict division between *formal* and *informal* somewhat arbitrary. It is precisely these informal practices that hold tremendous value, complemented by the daily routines of the residents. Incorporating these aspects into the design should be a priority.

As designers, we must shift away from rigid, universally applicable abstract concepts and embrace the diverse realities on the ground. Letting go of the need to categorize and instead embracing an open-minded approach, allows us to discover the nuanced middle

ground. This nuanced understanding becomes the key to appreciating informal settlements and their ways of living. They embody inherent strengths and unique communal dynamics that have evolved organically over time, deeply intertwined with the local culture.
By recognizing and integrating these strengths into contemporary housing design, we can bridge the gap between modern concepts and traditional practices.

They asked me to design a house,

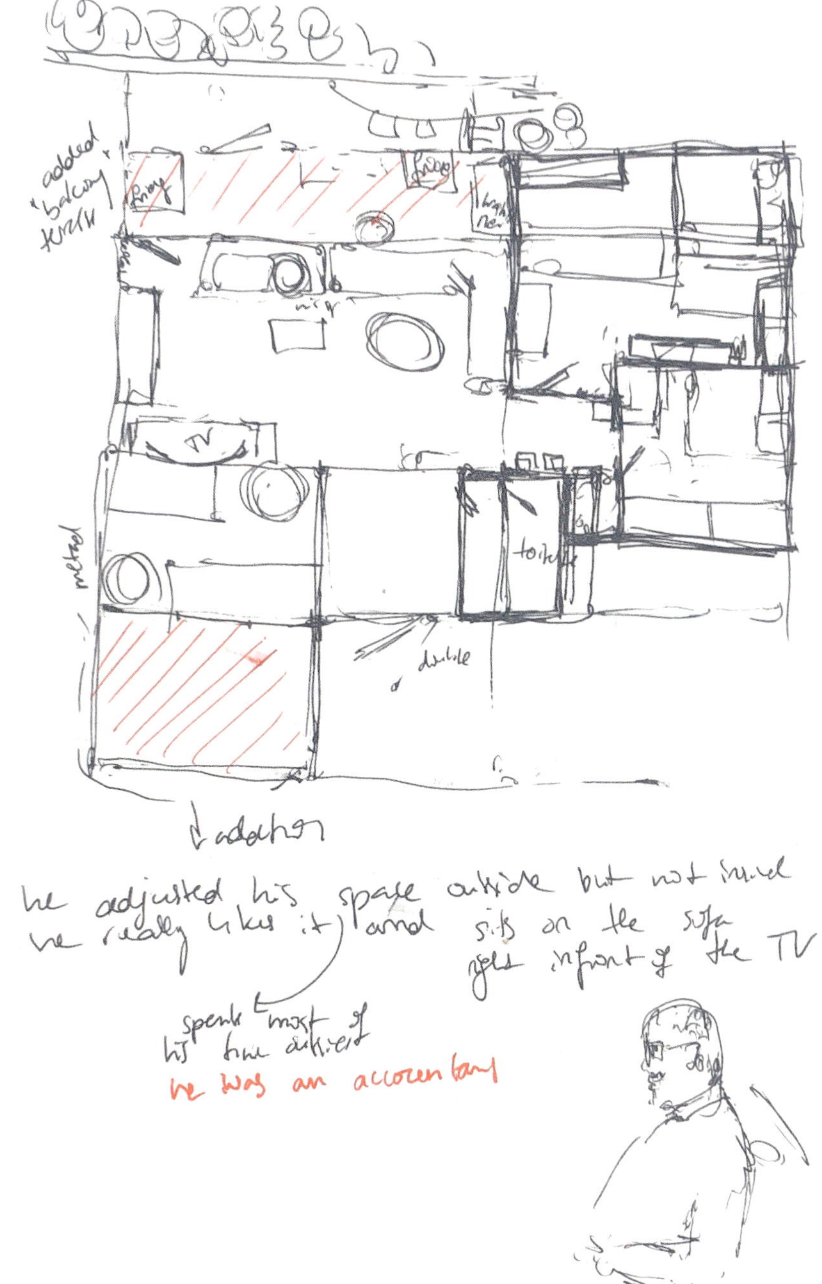

Figure 4
Floorplan. Sketch, Feven Gebeyehu Zeru, 2023. Source: personal archive. Copyright: Feven Gebeyehu Zeru.

FEVEN GEBEYEHU ZERU studied Architecture at the Technical University of Darmstadt and the Technical University of Delft. During her Master's studies, she focused on social housing and urban inclusivity, specifically addressing the challenges of affordable housing in Addis Ababa, Ethiopia. Currently working as an architectural designer in a Berlin-based office specializing in social housing, Feven is dedicated to creating adaptable, inclusive architecture that addresses the diverse needs of residents. Her goal is to further merge academic insights with practical applications, designing solutions that uplift marginalized voices and ensure representation and sensitivity in the built environment.

They asked me to design a house,

Beyond the *Polykatoikia*: Housing, Histories, and Futures

Conversation with Panos Dragonas

ILARIA AND GEORGINA ◣ Your professional and academic work is deeply connected to the topic of houses. What first sparked this interest, and how did your trajectory in this field begin?

PANOS ◣ I grew up in my father's architectural office, where he primarily designed apartment buildings in the 1970s and 1980s. I was part of the office from a very young age and I grew up in an environment where the main points of discussion were the Athens' *polykatoikia*[51] and the actual practices of building the Greek city. From the beginning, I understood the roles and limitations architects traditionally faced in the development process. After graduating and starting my career as an architect, I had limited opportunities to participate as a designer in the production of *polykatoikia* buildings. However, one of these projects gained significant recognition – *Polykatoikia in Pangrati* (2002). It became a well-known case, illustrating how *polykatoikia* evolved in the early 2000s, and was widely published in international architectural reviews, particularly during the 2004 Athens Olympic Games. The building stood out for its distinct approach, managing height and volumetric mass more effectively within the dense urban fabric of Athens. At the same time, I began working as an editor for leading architectural reviews in Greece. My role involved researching new publications and overseeing the publication of projects by young architects. This experience deepened my interest in the history of apartment buildings in Greece and led me to adopt a critical – though not negative – perspective on *polykatoikia.* I believe my generation was among the first to recognize its many positive aspects. In fact, I see *polykatoikia* as a success story – one that continues to shape the architectural identity of Greek cities.

GEORGINA ◣ What are your thoughts on the current state of *polykatoikia* as a housing typology? Do you believe it can still serve as an ideal living space – one that respects its residents, meets individual needs, and perhaps even inspires them?

PANOS ◣ To understand the current state of *polykatoikia*, we first need to acknowledge why it was a success story. I believe there are two key aspects, both of which can be visualized in a section drawing.
The first aspect concerns the way private and public uses were organically mixed within the *polykatoikia* structure. In the 1950s and 1960s, Athens lacked comprehensive urban planning. There were only basic regulations dictating where and how to build. As a result, society itself determined how public and commercial activities integrated within apartment buildings. This led to a highly effective mix of uses at the street level. Today, Athens is known for its vibrant street life, a direct outcome of this unplanned yet remarkable blending of residential and commercial functions.
The second aspect is more complex and, in my view, more compelling

51
Polykatoikia is a multi-storey apartment building, which appeared as a building type in Athens around 1910.

because it involves a significant social transformation. The rise of *polykatoikia* was driven by an urgent demand for housing as large numbers of people migrated from rural areas to Athens in search of shelter and employment. The construction industry became a major source of livelihood, reshaping the city's social structure. Comparing Athens in the 1930s and 1940s with the 1980s reveals a striking shift. In the 1940s, Greek society was highly polarized, with a stark divide between the upper and working classes. By the 1980s, apart from a small elite in the suburbs, most people – regardless of economic status – lived in *polykatoikia* apartments. These buildings existed across all neighborhoods, housing a diverse population. Within a single building, you might find a petit bourgeois family on the lower floors and an upper-middle-class household in the penthouse. Rather than creating a city of rigid class divisions, *polykatoikia* helped foster a predominantly lower-middle-class environment where different social groups coexisted. Its success lay in this soft vertical social stratification and its ability to bring together a once-fragmented population. So, what is happening today? While some of these dynamics persist, they are not as effective as before. One particularly interesting development is the arrival of new migrant populations in Greece since the 1990s. Many of the same buildings that once housed rural migrants in the 1950s and 1960s have, over the past two decades, become homes for new waves of migrants from Africa and Asia. However, this transition has not been as seamless. Unlike earlier migrations, integrating people from vastly different cultural backgrounds has proven more challenging. Nevertheless, this repetition of history is fascinating. Another major shift is the decline of lower-floor apartments. In many central areas, first- and second-floor units were abandoned over time, as they were less desirable living spaces in old *polykatoikia* buildings. Initially, these apartments were occupied by migrants from poorer countries. More recently, however, the rise of Airbnb and short-term rentals has brought another transformation, introducing a transient population into these buildings. Is this a success story? Not entirely, but it demonstrates the ongoing adaptability of *polykatoikia* – its ability to accommodate diverse populations and evolving uses.
Today's urban landscape is more complex. Some areas are thriving, while others are struggling with issues like gentrification. The process has been so gradual that displacement isn't always immediately visible, creating a sense that Athens remains resistant to change. However, it would be inaccurate to say that the city center has been fully gentrified – such a transformation is still unfolding and it will take time to materialize completely.

ILARIA ◣ When discussing informal cities, informality is often seen as a response to the challenges of neoliberal urban development – allowing housing to become a flexible, adaptable structure that residents can shape according to their needs. This approach enables cities to accommodate rapid urban growth while fostering a sense of agency among inhabitants. How, if at all, do you see

They asked me to design a house,

this concept relating to the *polykatoikia* phenomenon?

PANOS ◣ It depends on what you mean by "creating their own environment." Are you familiar with the *antiparochi* system? [52] Imagine owning a small piece of land in the center of Athens but lacking the funds to build a house. On the other hand, a developer may not own land but has the financial means and construction expertise. The *antiparochi* system allowed these two parties to collaborate in building a *polykatoikia* without direct monetary exchange. Once the construction was completed, the original landowner would receive a percentage of the apartments – typically 40% to 60% – as compensation. What is particularly interesting here is the role of the Greek state. In the 1950s, the Greek government recognized that large-scale social housing was not a viable option. Instead of undertaking direct public housing projects, the state allowed these private collaborations between landowners and developers, even offering them tax-free incentives. While the government did not directly profit from these arrangements, it provided a basic regulatory framework that covered aspects like building height, positioning, and essential construction guidelines. However, the focus was more on structural regulations rather than on broader urban planning, which allowed the phenomenon to grow organically, albeit without a cohesive vision for the city's development.

ILARIA ◣ Is *polykatoikia* a substitute for social housing, and was it developed without state investment?

PANOS ◣ Yes, *polykatoikia* can be considered a substitute for social housing, as it filled the gap left by the government's decision not to implement or support such programs. While it is difficult to conclusively prove the government's intentions, it is clear that no infrastructure existed for social housing development at the time.
The conservative government, freshly emerged from the civil war (1946-1949) between communists and conservatives, likely feared creating concentrated working-class neighborhoods. They were more interested in building a city that integrated different social groups, rather than segregating them. Concentrating the working class could have bolstered their political power, potentially making the fear of a communist uprising more real.
As for state investment, the situation is nuanced. It is tempting to view *polykatoikia* as a bottom-up phenomenon, where the people built their own homes without state intervention. This is partly true – the buildings were primarily developed through collaborations between landowners and small developers, not large construction firms. These small-scale developers worked incrementally, often constructing one *polykatoikia* at a time in the same neighborhoods. As this process spread, it allowed the city to gradually

52
The *antiparochi* system was enabled by the 1929 law of horizontal ownership and according to it a landowner could turn over the plot to a constructor, usually a small scale construction company, in order to build a multi-storey apartment block receiving in exchange an agreed number of apartments in the finished building. cohabathens.org/portfolio/antiparochi-land-for-flat/

replicate itself across Athens.
However, it would be too simplistic to view this entirely as a bottom-up system. While the state did not directly finance or construct the buildings, it played a crucial role in regulating how the *polykatoikia* was developed. The state maintained control by setting building standards, zoning laws, and construction guidelines, essentially shaping the framework within which this private development occurred.

GEORGINA ◣ We'd love to learn more about your role as an educator. Could you share some insights into the architectural design studios you teach in? Since some of these studios focus on housing, could you walk us through how you prepare the briefs for those projects?

PANOS ◣ A few years ago, the brief for the studio focused on the adaptive reuse of old *polykatoikia* buildings, particularly those from the 1960s and 1970s. I was keen to explore the future of these structures and what should be done with them. I had a clear perspective on what should be preserved and what needed to change. First, I believe these buildings should be preserved, as demolishing them would be both costly and environmentally problematic. Most of these buildings are likely to stand for many years, but there are certainly issues that need addressing. Originally, they were designed for a traditional nuclear family, a model that no longer represents the only family structure. It's important to remember that when the *antiparochi* system was implemented, the nuclear family was the dominant social model. In 1960s and 1970s Greece, it was difficult to survive without being married with children.
I believe there's a biopolitical aspect to the *antiparochi* system – it didn't just create buildings, it also shaped lifestyles, following a conservative, Western nuclear family model. This ideal was not just encouraged by architecture but also by the film industry of the time, which often depicted this lifestyle inside the *polykatoikia.* This influence wasn't incidental; it was part of the broader "Americanization" of Greek society.

One key question we addressed with the students was what the *polykatoikia* of the future might look like – how the apartment typology could evolve to cater to more diverse living arrangements beyond just nuclear families. We also examined the lack of communal spaces. The *polykatoikia* celebrates the private sphere, with public functions often pushed into private spaces by necessity, but communal areas were minimal and problematic. Roof gardens were underutilized, open spaces were abandoned, and circulation areas were often inadequate. Improving these common spaces became a central design challenge. Another issue we explored was the aesthetic of the *polykatoikia.* While I appreciate the simplicity and repetition of private elements in the facade, I don't think this will hold up in the future. These questions formed the core of the studio's focus on the adaptive reuse of *polykatoikia* buildings.

ILARIA ◣ How did the students respond to this challenge? Were they fully aware of the complexities behind these typologies?

They asked me to design a house,

PANOS ◣ I think it's important to understand why a critical perspective on *polykatoikia* has developed over time. In terms of design, I aimed to keep the studio open and exploratory, rather than pragmatic – more of a space for innovative ideas. For instance, some students proposed creating larger, open areas for vertical gardens by demolishing parts of the building, or designing a vertical playground for children, which could then integrate a new communal space. Personally, I favored a more conceptual approach, which proved to be quite successful. Although I haven't used this brief in the past three years, I might bring it back in the future. More recently, my focus has shifted to the transformation of apartments in light of new technologies. This shift stems from observing how digital spaces, media, and platforms like Zoom have increasingly invaded our domestic environments.

GEORGINA ◣ How do you approach the concept of domesticity in light of the growing influence of technology? Can we still preserve the sense of familiarity and comfort that defines a home, even as new technologies reshape the way we use these spaces? Is this emotional connection something you consider in the design process, or do you focus more on the functionality of these spaces?

PANOS ◣ That's a great question, and it's one I approach with a blend of realism and detail. For example, I consider what kind of furniture works best for incorporating technologies like VR systems. The television, for instance, was the one object that truly transformed apartments, becoming the focal point of living rooms for many years. Interestingly, architects often avoid designing around the TV's position, perhaps because we're uncomfortable with its dominance, but we also know it's been a central feature in many homes. Over the past decade or so, this focus has shifted toward networking devices and more interconnected technologies. So, how will this evolve? What new spaces and furniture will emerge as part of this ongoing reinvention of domesticity? I don't have all the answers, but I focus on raising these important questions in my studios with students, encouraging them to think critically about how these technologies will continue to reshape home environments.

ILARIA ◣ Your teaching is deeply influenced by external societal factors, which is essential. How do you balance designing for the present while also envisioning the future in your approach?

PANOS ◣ The key is to think about how we engage with the future. In recent years, I've focused a lot on the concept of the future, conducting research into the work of visionary Greek architects from the 1960s, who developed unique approaches to future-oriented design. What I've realized is that it's not so much about predicting the future, but about understanding how we can shape it. The future is not a fixed idea; it's something we must actively participate in creating, and it requires a flexible approach. The future is, in a sense, a collaborative project. While ideologies are always significant, the

way we engage with the future - and the flexibility we bring to that process - are key elements in shaping it.
In the past year, my research has centered on Greek visionary architects like Constantinos Doxiadis (1913-1975) and Takis Zenetos (1926-1977). Doxiadis' work is particularly fascinating because of his exploration of the future and his systematic approach to anticipating its possibilities. Zenetos, on the other hand, delved into how technology would influence the future. Both architects offer invaluable insights into how the future could be understood and designed - not just as a distant idea, but as a real, evolving project we can help guide.

GEORGINA ◣ How could the *polykatoikia* evolve in the future to address emerging challenges, such as urban gentrification, while also meeting the universal need for a home that feels familiar and connected to domestic life?

PANOS ◣ I don't have a specific answer, but I believe it's more about asking the right, nuanced questions. In the context of Greece, this becomes even more interesting because the country has historically been, and to some extent still is, quite conservative - especially when it comes to design and architectural practices. While there has been progress, convincing developers to allocate space for communal areas remains a challenge. Incorporating new ideas, like those commonly seen in cities like Barcelona, still feels difficult and often meets resistance in Greece.

GEORGINA ◣ As a tutor, do you believe the younger generation of students has the potential to shift this status quo and pursue more radical solutions?

PANOS ◣ This has long been a challenge in Greek architecture: while there has always been great work, truly radical architecture has been rare. This was true in the 1960s, with only a few exceptions, and it remains the case today. Despite having many talented designers, Greece doesn't seem to produce the level of radical thinking or originality that you might find in places like Portugal. One explanation for this could be the overwhelming influence of tourism on the built environment. The entire country is being shaped around tourism interests, leading to repetitive and uninspired developments. To understand this issue more deeply, we might need to consider sociology. Personally, I'm not overly optimistic about the future. The vast majority of students are focused on secure jobs in established architectural firms. In my studio, however, I encourage students to see each design project as a narrative, as a way of articulating how they envision a small piece of the world in the future. I ask them to develop a coherent story, one that defines not only their practice but also their position in the world. I believe that's a crucial starting point - helping students understand their own positionality and how their designs can be part of a larger narrative that connects their work with the broader societal context.

They asked me to design a house,

Figure 1
Polykatoikia at Pagkrati. Panos Dragonas, 2002. Photo Credits: Charalambos Louizides. Source: Panos Dragonas. Copyright: Panos Dragonas.

Figure 2
Yorgos Genovezos, Lambros Faraj, ePolykatoikia (Architectural Design 7 studio project at the Department of Architecture, University of Patras. Tutor: Panos Dragonas), 2023-24. Source: Panos Dragonas. Copyright: Panos Dragonas.

Panos asked them to design a home

PANOS DRAGONAS is an architect, curator, and Professor of Architecture and Urban Design at the University of Patras. He studied in Athens (NTUA) and New York (GSAPP, Columbia University) as a Fulbright Scholar. In 2020, he founded Dragonas. Studio in Athens. His award-winning design work has been featured in international exhibitions and publications. He was joint commissioner and curator of *Made in Athens* (Venice Biennale, 2012) and co-curator of *Tomorrows* (Athens, 2017; Nantes, 2019), among other exhibitions. His research focuses on the transformation of Greek cities and the intersections of architecture, cinema, and modern urban life, including ongoing studies on Athenian modernity and Takis Zenetos' *Electronic Urbanism.*

They asked me to design a house,

Dichotomy of Dwelling

Ines Glowania

Domesticity has changed drastically in the last couple of years. The pandemic added a new function to our homes: the office. Our permanent residence became a hybrid space between work and leisure. In addition, the new flexibility of less fixed working environments enabled the evolution of a new species of workers. The "digital nomad" is a person who works while moving between places. The term became known (especially) through Tsugio Makimoto and David Manners, who foresee in their homonymous book[53] that digital technology will enable humans to go back to a nomadic lifestyle. Anyhow, with these two new ways of living – the hybrid home and the world-is-my-home – the idea of dwelling has been shifted. Homes became either an all-in-one space or non-existent. It is uncertain whether we need a permanent home. It is, however, certain that we need shelter. But how much space do we actually need?

53
Tsugio Makimoto and David Manners, *Digital Nomad* (New York: Wiley, 1997).

54
Le Corbusier, *Towards a New Architecture* (Mineola, NY: Dover Publications, 2021), 107.

This question was central to modernist architects, who aimed to design functional, efficient, and geometric houses and interiors. Among them, Le Corbusier, the renowned French architect and pioneer of modern architecture, famously declared in his seminal book *Towards a New Architecture* that "The house is a machine for living in."[54] This statement suggests that architects, like engineers, should approach design with precision – integrating mathematical calculation, economic logic, and principles of industrial production. To ground architecture in mathematical reasoning, Le Corbusier developed an anthropometric scale of proportion in 1948 called *The Modulor*. This measurement system was based on the dimensions of the human body, referencing the "standard" human height. Le Corbusier's concept drew inspiration from Leonardo da Vinci's Vitruvian Man, which itself was based on the writings of the ancient Roman architect Vitruvius. These interwoven influences highlight the enduring quest for harmony between human proportions and architectural design throughout history.

Le Corbusier designed *Le Cabanon* on the basis of the Modulor in 1952: a minimum cell (3.66 x 3.66 meters x 2.26 meters high) on the French seaside that reminds us of the function and ergonomics of a ship's cabin. If we ask how much space we actually need, *Le Cabanon* might be Le Corbusier's answer. However, when a house is a machine for living, and our space is determined by rules, reason, and function, are we then merely gear wheels within the architecture that shelters us? Who do we become when a house is a machine?

Today, much of Western architecture is deeply rooted in modernist principles: mass production, standardization, functionality, and the emphasis on simple, clean forms. In his book *The Modulor*, Le Corbusier wrote: "To take possession of space is the first gesture of the living, men and beasts, plants and clouds, the fundamental manifestation of equilibrium and permanence. The first proof of existence is to occupy space."[55] The way we inhabit space defines how we exist. That is why we need to reflect on the machine we are living in. *The Modulor* notably excluded female measurements, exemplifying how women and their needs were often overlooked in modernist architecture. But wait – that's not entirely true. Women did get the *Frankfurt Kitchen,* designed by Margarete Schütte-Lihotzky in 1926. This kitchen was carefully crafted around the movements, bodies, and practical needs of women, revolutionizing domestic efficiency. So, thank you, modernism – for the token acknowledgment, at least. Surely, gender roles were different at the time, and we needed to go through some waves of feminism to come as far as we have today (not far enough, though). However, the Frankfurt kitchen shows us how controlling and socially or politically engraving architecture is. Or how Simone de Beauvoir, a French social theorist and feminist, phrased it in her book *The Second Sex*: "Woman is shut up in a kitchen or in a boudoir, and astonishment is expressed that her horizon is limited. Her wings are clipped, and it is found deplorable that she cannot fly..."[56] De Beauvoir meant the kitchen as a space in general rather than its specific architecture. But when the space is also designed for women, it is like sugarcoating a rotten apple.

55
Le Corbusier, *The Modulor* (London: Faber & Faber, 1961), 30.

56
Simone de Beauvoir, *The Second Sex* (New York: Vintage Classics, 1956), 574.

Times have changed, and we need to evaluate these spatial imaginaries of modernist beliefs and stereotypes – especially considering our new ways of living. Our physical infrastructure is now interwoven with a digital one. How is *The Modulor* (as a symbol of modernist architecture) still up-to-date if our physical bodies

They asked me to design a house,

have virtually extended? Is there a need for a new human scale – one that includes this new and digital body of ours and one that is of course not misogynistic? New technological achievements inspired Le Corbusier to rethink architecture. In his book *The Modulor*, he says: "The conclusion to be drawn from it is this: that everything is becoming – indeed, has already become – interdependent. Demands are shifting and conquering new spaces."[57] Here, Le Corbusier refers to modern aviation and globalization. However, his statement fits today's spirit and goes beyond. This time, demands are not only about "conquering new spaces" but about becoming a new space – the digital. A profound societal change comes with this interconnectedness. We have all the freedom to move and also no need to move at all. How do our rooms, houses, streets, and cities create space for this dichotomy of inhabiting? Le Corbusier's idea of micro-living might work for digital nomads and thoughts of a new hospitality, but what does a home look like for someone who will never leave the house? What becomes obvious is the need for a radical rethinking of architecture. New requirements and realities demand new thoughts and implementations. In the end, there are just three questions left: "Who will rethink architecture?", "What will it look like?", and "Are you staying home or making the world your home?"

57 Le Corbusier, *The Modulor*, 18.

INES GLOWANIA is a research-based designer and writer with a MA in Information Design from Design Academy Eindhoven. In her practice she investigates topics of art, design, architecture, culture and politics to create installations or written text. In 2020, she was part of the Bauhaus Lab, a resVearch residency by Bauhaus Dessau and later became co-author of the book "A Concrete for the Other Half." Additionally, she writes for magazines like DAMN Magazine (Belgium) and Disegno (UK).

They asked me to design a house,

Performing the Home: Gender, Space, and Collective Practice

Conversation with Edit Collective

ILARIA AND GEORGINA How did your work and research on domesticity start?

ALICE After graduating from the Royal College of Art (RCA) in London, we returned to our commercial architecture jobs, only to quickly realize that the workplaces didn't provide the freedom to explore the ideas we had developed at the RCA. While the RCA had pushed us to think radically about spaces, the reality of our new jobs felt at odds with that same creative and innovative approach.

SOPHIE It all began informally, sparked by a casual idea to participate in an open call. Alberte and Hannah had both conducted in-depth research on domesticity and gender during their time at university, while Alice had explored similar themes in her undergraduate studies. Together, we shared a deep interest in examining the political hierarchies embedded in the design and construction of domestic spaces. The first open call we responded to was for Oslo Architecture Triennale in 2019, which led to the creation of the *Gross Domestic Product* (GDP) project.

ALICE We were focused on exploring the spaces of the home as made up theatrical sets – how gender roles are performed within it and how objects become props in the performance.

SOPHIE Examining how gender and hierarchies are constructed in society reveals that these dynamics are often concentrated within the domestic environment. However, these political and social structures extend beyond the home and are also deeply embedded in the city. Our research often overlaps with these themes, exploring how they manifest in urban, public, and communal spaces.

ILARIA Could you elaborate on the connection between the public and domestic spheres? In what ways do you see these two spaces overlapping, and how do you approach these intersections in your work?

ALICE The domestic sphere we researched, even if limited to the western and westernised world, is relatable to many, living in very similar kinds of spaces. We started by examining the hierarchies within the home, such as the distinction between the master bedroom and the single bedroom, or who sits at the table, who serves, and who is excluded from these rituals. Our exploration then extended from the domestic into the public realm, investigating how domestic activities, like laundry, were once publicly expressed through communal practices – many of which have now faded. We also focused on public toilets, delving into the broader societal implications of these spaces and questioning who is allowed to participate in public life, and who remains excluded.

GEORGINA One time, during my PhD committee meeting, I was asked why it's so crucial to approach domesticity. To me, it's important because domesticity is multifaceted and resonates with everyone in some way – everyone has their own version of it. On a broader scale, domesticity extends beyond the home and can be reflected in public and urban environments as well.

SOPHIE Yes, exactly. Domesticity is so relatable because it's such a personal experience. The way we organize our homes is shaped by deep-rooted social and political structures, and these norms eventually become so ingrained that we accept them as natural. A big part of this is tied to the nuclear family model, which is especially prevalent in Western societies, and it influences who is expected to contribute financially or perform domestic duties. We're really interested in investigating this further – looking at how reproductive and domestic labor is often invisible or undervalued, and who ends up doing the care work. These issues aren't confined to the home; they permeate urban life as well. Take, for instance, the cleaners we see working during the night in public spaces and offices. This is a clear reflection of broader labor dynamics and the social hierarchies that come with it.

ILARIA In the architectural job market, there's often a sharp distinction between how we approach design in public versus domestic spaces, and this divide can sometimes feel like an obstacle when trying to connect the two. We aim to bridge that gap, but I often struggle to find people who truly grasp the importance of this interconnectedness. How has your experience been with this challenge? What kind of feedback or reactions do you usually encounter when you bring up these topics?

SOPHIE When we discuss how home design is often imposed on us, shaping societal structures, people can become defensive. Many don't want to accept that the way their homes are designed is largely influenced by pre-established norms and conventions. There's a strong desire to believe that their living spaces reflect personal choice and individuality, rather than recognizing the extent to which these designs are prescribed by external forces.

GEORGINA Can you describe how your work process is structured? How do you approach research? How do you manage to sustain yourself in this field? What types of projects do you typically pursue, or do they come to you? Do you follow a particular guiding concept or idea?

ALICE We mainly receive commissions, but we are fortunate to have other sources of income: we work multiple jobs. This means that if a particular commission doesn't align with our values as a collective, we have the freedom to decline it.

SOPHIE The first open call we participated in was a self-directed exploration of our interests. Following that, we began receiving commissions that aligned with our approach and exploration of spaces. Over time, people have come to understand our focus and the areas we are passionate about intervening in.

ILARIA Having worked with specific items from the domestic environment, how do you convey the personal, individual relationships people have with these objects while presenting them within a collective context?

ALICE The goal of the Gross Domestic Product was not to offer a design solution to the gendered issue of housework,

They asked me to design a house,

but was rather an object meant to be thought provoking and at the same time performative. We wanted it to be fully functioning and to be able to be used and 'performed' by visitors of the exhibition.

SOPHIE We also developed a sort of instruction by crafting a fictional history for the object, with the intention of legitimizing it and prompting people to question whether it could have truly existed. For instance, drawing inspiration from the history of the hoover vacuum, we created a narrative about the designer's daughter collaborating with him to design the GDP and taking inspiration from communal laundries. This use of fictional narratives helps to challenge the notion that the way we live today is somehow natural or inevitable. It opens up space to explore alternative possibilities – imagining what could have been if history, especially in architecture, had taken a different course.

We rely heavily on storytelling, crafting fictional scenarios to provoke new ways of thinking. This approach reveals how the narratives we live by are themselves constructed, while also validating alternative narratives as equally legitimate. It's proven to be a powerful tool for reimagining how we interact with and inhabit our environments, encouraging a more flexible, creative approach to design and the spaces we occupy.

ALICE We also work a lot with editing pop culture images. We use different ways to get people to jump into something that is recognizable.

GEORGINA What project are you currently working on, and what are your next steps moving forward?

SOPHIE In terms of how we project ourselves, we take it step by step. We try to keep Edit Collective quite fluid, we have been lucky to have a steady stream of people coming to us with interesting things. Recently, we all got into teaching which was inherently rewarding but also a good stage to explore things. We were able to run our own unit at LSA, London School of Architecture, this year. We created the brief and explored it with the students. It was both a learning and a research process for us. We also have some public space projects coming. Right now we are working on a public realm project co-designed with young people of Somers Town, an area in central London. It's an intriguing way to approach the representation of different groups in the design of public spaces. Many young women, for instance, are often defined by what they're perceived to need in these spaces. We've been fortunate to facilitate conversations with them, delving into how we can truly co-design in a feminist way, ensuring that different voices are heard and represented. It's something we continually strive to embody in our work. We often find ourselves working on a diverse range of projects that allow us to co-design with local community groups – whether through quick-turnaround research, exhibitions, or permanent installations. It's a great balance of practical application and creative experimentation, helping us explore and test ideas in real-world contexts.

ILARIA It seems that you explore your topics through various mediums, including teaching, which you mentioned is an enriching way to initiate these conversations in an educational setting. Both of us have struggled with feeling misunderstood in similar environments. How do you approach these methodologies, and how do you introduce the values central to your practice within your teaching?

ALICE It's different for everyone. I teach first-year architecture students at Birmingham City University. The approach to teaching is different compared to Masters as there is less flexibility to shape a brief. With my students, the focus is on helping them understand the basics of design through inclusive principles.

ILARIA I think it's really beneficial because it allows you to break away from the traditional first-year brief. You can approach things differently, giving students a fresh perspective and allowing for more flexibility in how they engage with the design process.

SOPHIE I completely agree. Working with undergraduates is such a unique opportunity, especially when you can guide them toward understanding how spaces can be designed inclusively. Inclusivity was not a priority when we studied at undergraduate level. When we were designing the brief for our unit, we had to really deconstruct some of the traditional aspects of architectural education and practice. It was a lot of work to challenge those mainstream ideas, but being able to do that with undergraduates is incredibly powerful – you can make a lasting impact on how they think about and approach design. Alberte and I led a workshop based on a game we created for an exhibition, "Domestic Consequences". The game had students reflect on how the design of our homes is often imposed by specific familiar structures. We had students design homes for alternative family structures using pop culture references, like the Kardashians and the Spice Girls. It was incredible to see some students react with, "That just blew my mind!" – because it made them think about things they'd never considered before. Teaching offers such a valuable opportunity for intervention. We also give lectures at architecture practices in London, and many people have expressed surprise, saying things like, "I never realized how deeply politics are embedded in the design of something as basic as a floor plan." It's so rewarding to see those moments of realization and critical reflection.

They asked me to design a house,

Edit asked them to design a home

EDIT is a feminist architecture collective working on design and research projects. We are interested in the enduring biases and hierarchies embedded in the built environment and we have designed projects spanning from objects and film to exhibition design and public spaces. We are architects, project managers, set designers, tutors and researchers and have combined experience across projects of all scales and stages. Our work has been exhibited at the 2019 Oslo Architecture Triennale, MAXXI in Rome, the Design Museum, Akademie der Kunste and during the London Design Festival, among others. Our clients include the Barbican Centre, Science Gallery London, Camden Council, Farrell Centre and People's Museum Somers Town. Edit was nominated for Manifestos: Architecture for a New Generation, highlighting emerging voices shaping architecture in London, and have recently been featured in the RIBA Journal Future Winners, and Architects' Journal Architectural Antagonists.

They asked me to design a house,

Under the Carpet

Davide Tommaso Ferrando
Kevin Shu LAI
la-di-da
Michele Rinaldi
Nicholas Korody
Georgina Pantazopoulou

INTRODUCTION

In an increasingly interconnected world, digital technologies are profoundly reshaping the concept of home and domesticity by transforming the ways we inhabit, experience, and organize domestic spaces. This chapter delves into the evolving understanding of domesticity, exploring how homes have transformed into complex sites of performance, pedagogy, care, and political agency, shaped by social, technological, and economic forces.

Davide Tommaso Ferrando's reflections on *post-domesticity*, where homes have become part of a vast digital theater, invites us to think about spaces that are zones of performance: content houses, Airbnb apartments, gaming dens, where the self is constantly curated for others. In our conversation, questions are raised about the shifting role of architecture in mediating identity and on how domesticity is entangled with visibility and production in the digital age.

Extending this interrogation of domestic space, Kevin Shu Lai presents the transformation of a soon-to-be-demolished apartment in Zurich into a site of collective learning and unlearning. Through shared meals, conversations, and experiments, the home is reimagined as a pedagogical platform, suggesting that education and design are inseparable from the spaces in which they unfold, and that domesticity itself can be a method for rethinking community and belonging.

Architects Laura van Santen and Diederik de Koning (la-di-da) present a grounded approach to affordable housing, emphasizing empathy, sustainability, and the long-term social impact of design decisions. To them, to design a home with care means questioning every step: from how we engage clients, to the way we source materials and measure value beyond aesthetics

Michele Rinaldi's analysis of Rosa Menni Giolli's 1933 article La Casa Di Una Donna Sola (*'A Single Woman's Home'*) situates gender,

They asked me to design a house,

housing, and modernity within the rise of fascism in 1930s Italy. Giolli's advocacy for housing solutions for single women reveals how domestic space shaped women's autonomy and intersected with broader struggles for gender equality.

Nicholas Korody's research into domesticity highlights its ties to labor, consumption, and self-expression, particularly as shaped by women yet politically and economically marginalized. Through discussions of the sex industry, online intimacy, and decoration, he reframes the home as both a product and site of social transformation.

Georgina Pantazopoulou calls for an intersectional feminist approach to interior architecture. She critiques an architectural education that privileges technical mastery over the lived, emotional, and political realities of domestic life. Home is more than a functional container; it is a site where identities are negotiated, relationships are shaped, and power is contested.

Across these contributions, domestic spaces are no longer confined to physical interiors but extend into digital and speculative realms. Domesticity is presented here as a way to reconfigure how we relate to one another and to the spaces we inhabit. By centering lived experience, affective labor, and material conditions, the authors and practitioners in this chapter reveal domesticity as a critical site of design, one that is inseparable from broader questions of access, sex, race, agency, and belonging in a rapidly shifting world.

Under the carpet,
lifting its edge, revealing the quite hidden lives and labors

beneath.

They asked me to design a house,

The Content Room:
Post-Domestic Interiors and Digital Subjectivities
Conversation with Davide Tommaso Ferrando

ILARIA AND GEORGINA ◯ How did your research on post-domesticity start?

DAVIDE ◯ My initial exploration of this topic began within the realm of didactics. My path as an educator has been somewhat varied: I moved from Innsbruck, where I taught in the Department of Architectural Theory and History, to Bolzano, where I now teach in the Faculty of Design and Arts. In Innsbruck, in 2016, I started researching how digital media are transforming architectural culture at large. The first course I taught there, "Other Media, Other Architecture," focused on the cultural shifts brought about by digital technologies in architecture.
From that course onward, we consistently had at least one student per studio who chose a topic related to the transformation of domestic space through the Internet. In this way, the subject itself began to take shape during the conversations with my students. The rise of Airbnb in 2016 became a key point of discussion, prompting critical reflections on technology's impact on urbanism and the transformation of domestic spaces into temporary commercial assets, in which individual rooms can be rented out to host specific functions.
A recurrent reference for this first exploration was a rather intriguing film by Ila Bêka and Louise Lemoine, titled *Selling Dreams.* First presented at the 2016 Oslo Architecture Triennale, the story follows an Airbnb owner who doesn't have a personal home but instead lives in hotels, managing multiple properties. To create a sense of authenticity, the owner installs cameras and furnishes each apartment uniquely, crafting diverse narratives for each space. Exploring the paradoxes connected to the fictional forms of domesticity that can be generated by digital platforms, the film was a fiction itself.
In 2019, a flatmate introduced me to the concept of "gaming houses," where teams rent flats to play video games 24/7 for profit. This led me to explore the transformative impact of apps and live streaming on domestic spaces. Not only are apps transforming the way domestic spaces are inhabited, but live streaming has also become one of the major agents of post-domesticity. The documentary *People's Republic of Desire*, directed by Hao Wu, explores China's live-streaming culture, where private rooms are transformed into content studios. This phenomenon introduces a new dimension to domestic typologies, transforming rooms into content studios that serve to amplify and expand the streamer's persona.
Similarly, the Netflix documentary *Hype House* focuses on a California mansion inhabited by eighteen TikTokers, where creators gather to produce videos together and share followers, amplifying their collective reach. The documentary unveils a dual narrative, portraying the content house as both a creative hub and, ironically, a labor camp disguised as a luxury residence. The constant staging of domestic moments blurs the boundary between private and public life, fundamentally altering the traditional concept of a home. As Walter Benjamin once said, the house is the bourgeois interior where you present yourself to society and find shelter from it. In contrast, in the content house, the home

is no longer a refuge. Instead, it becomes a transparent site where individuals fully immerse themselves in society, transforming into spectacles for the public eye. They cease to find shelter and instead become part of the very mechanism of capital production and value extraction. For me, this represents a paradigmatic shift, which is why I continue to explore these topics.

GEORGINA ◠ I've been reflecting on *Glitch Feminism: A Manifesto* by Legacy Russell, particularly its exploration of how those who feel unsafe or disconnected in their domestic environments might find familiarity and belonging in the digital sphere. Russell portrays the digital world as a space of resistance and transformation, where individuals can reimagine their realities and craft new worlds. This raises a compelling question: In what ways can the digital sphere foster genuine feelings of familiarity or intimacy for those who lack comfort in their physical homes?

DAVIDE ◠ Even when domestic spaces are opened to the public through webcams and microphones, the individual retains a degree of control. By replacing embodied, face-to-face communication with abstract, mediated interactions, a dynamic emerges where authenticity can be exchanged between performer and observer – but always within the boundaries set by the individual. Everything mediated by a webcam, whether consciously or unconsciously, becomes a staged performance.

This dynamic is twofold. On the one hand, there's control: you decide what to reveal and what to withhold. On the other hand, performing for the camera begins to shape and construct your persona, blurring the line between your true self and the version curated for the audience. This idea resonates with Lacan's concept of "extimacy," which challenges the traditional understanding of intimacy. Rather than defining intimacy as a purely private, inner sphere distinct from the external world, Lacan suggests that the inner and outer realms are interconnected and mutually constitutive, with no definitive boundary between them. Webcams do more than document domestic spaces – they fictionalize them, actively producing rather than merely reproducing or broadcasting these environments. Not all streamed domestic spaces are meticulously composed; some purposefully maintain untidiness to evoke a sense of authenticity over an overtly staged presentation. In both cases, these kinds of hypermediatized interiors are highly curated. The performative use of domestic imagery extends beyond private life into the public sphere, often serving as a narrative tool. For instance, political figures like American presidents, Queen Elizabeth, and Silvio Berlusconi have leveraged domestic imagery to reinforce their personal identities and expand their public narratives. Berlusconi's 1994 political debut notably involved a staged domestic setting within an improvised TVstudio opened inside of a tool shack, whose composition and selection of elements was meant to evoke familiarity and trust. This use of domesticity taps into the broader appeal of intimacy as

They asked me to design a house,

Figure *1*
The streaming room of Chinese singer Shen Man. Still image taken from the documentary *People's Republic of Desire* (2018) by Chinese American director Hao Wu.

Figure *2*
The living room of the gaming house of American eSport Team Cloud9 (2019). Still image taken from the video *Cloud9 CS:GO HyperX Gaming House Tour 2019* on the YouTube channel 'HyperX'.

Figure *3*
The entry into politics of Silvio Berlusconi. January 25, 1994. Still image taken from the video *La Discesa in Campo - 26 gennaio 1994* on the YouTube channel 'lastoriadisilvio'.

Figure *4*
Three still images taken from different videos on the Hype House TikTok channel.

They asked me to design a house,

a valuable asset. *Cold Intimacies: The Making of Emotional Capitalism* provides an insightful exploration of how digital communication has commodified intimacy, transforming it into a tool for connection, persuasion, and influence in both personal and public contexts.

ILARIA ◯ I studied in the faculty of Interior Design with an education based on modernism. I found that many topics discussed in our conversation were not covered in my educational experience. Have you encountered a similar situation?

DAVIDE ◯ I can't speak for the entirety of architectural education, as I'm not familiar with all aspects. However, based on my experience, I can confirm that, at least in the institutions where I have taught recently, proper education on the political dimensions of interior design is still confined to a sort of academic niche, particularly within traditional architectural curricula. The discourse on the political complexity of domesticity has been ongoing for a while, and there are many magazines and books that document the relevance and richness of the topic, but it's to me unclear how deeply it is integrated into teaching. Probably because despite technological innovations such as social media influencing domestic practices, the physical layer of domestic space remains largely unchanged, still rooted in tradition and resilience. From this point of view, the recent emergence of a new kind of room, the so called "content room", represents a significant paradigm shift, altering spatial production within domestic spaces.

I believe that we currently find ourselves in a transitional phase, contemplating the birth of new domestic spaces that are meant to accommodate evolving practices. The fact that IKEA is now producing furniture specifically conceived for gaming is quite significant from this point of view. Nonetheless, we should refrain from adopting the modernist vision that if society changes, then architectural form should change. Or even worse, that we have to change architectural form to change society. What we can do, for a start, is examine, describe and possibly criticise the new everyday practices that contemporary domestic space is producing, under the influence of digital communication technologies, and the new subjectivities that are emerging from them.

DAVIDE TOMMASO FERRANDO is an architecture critic and curator, particularly interested in the intersections between architecture, city and digital media. Master in Advanced Architectural Design at ETSA Madrid and Ph.D in Architecture and Building Design at Politecnico di Torino, he is Research Fellow at the Faculty of Design and Art of the Free University of Bozen Bolzano Davide is an invited lecturer in universities such as Aarhus School of Architecture, IUAV Venezia, The Berlage Delft and Architectural Association London. Together with Daniel Tudor Munteanu, since 2016 Davide is the founder and curator of the Unfolding Pavilion: an expanding curatorial project that pops-up on the occasion of the Venice Architecture Biennale. Davide and Daniel are also the curators of the 2022 edition of Beta – Timisoara Architecture Biennial, and of its main exhibition *Another Breach in the Wall.* Davide is a contributor to “The Architectural Review” and his writings are published in magazines such as “Log”, “Casabella”, “Bauwelt” and “Volume.” Davide is the author of *The City in the Image* (Vibok Works, 2018), *Another Breach in the Wall* (Solitude Project, 2022), *Building Stories* (Letteraventidue, 2023) and *City of Legends: Stanze, Web e Social Network* (Krisis Publishing, 2024).

They asked me to design a house,

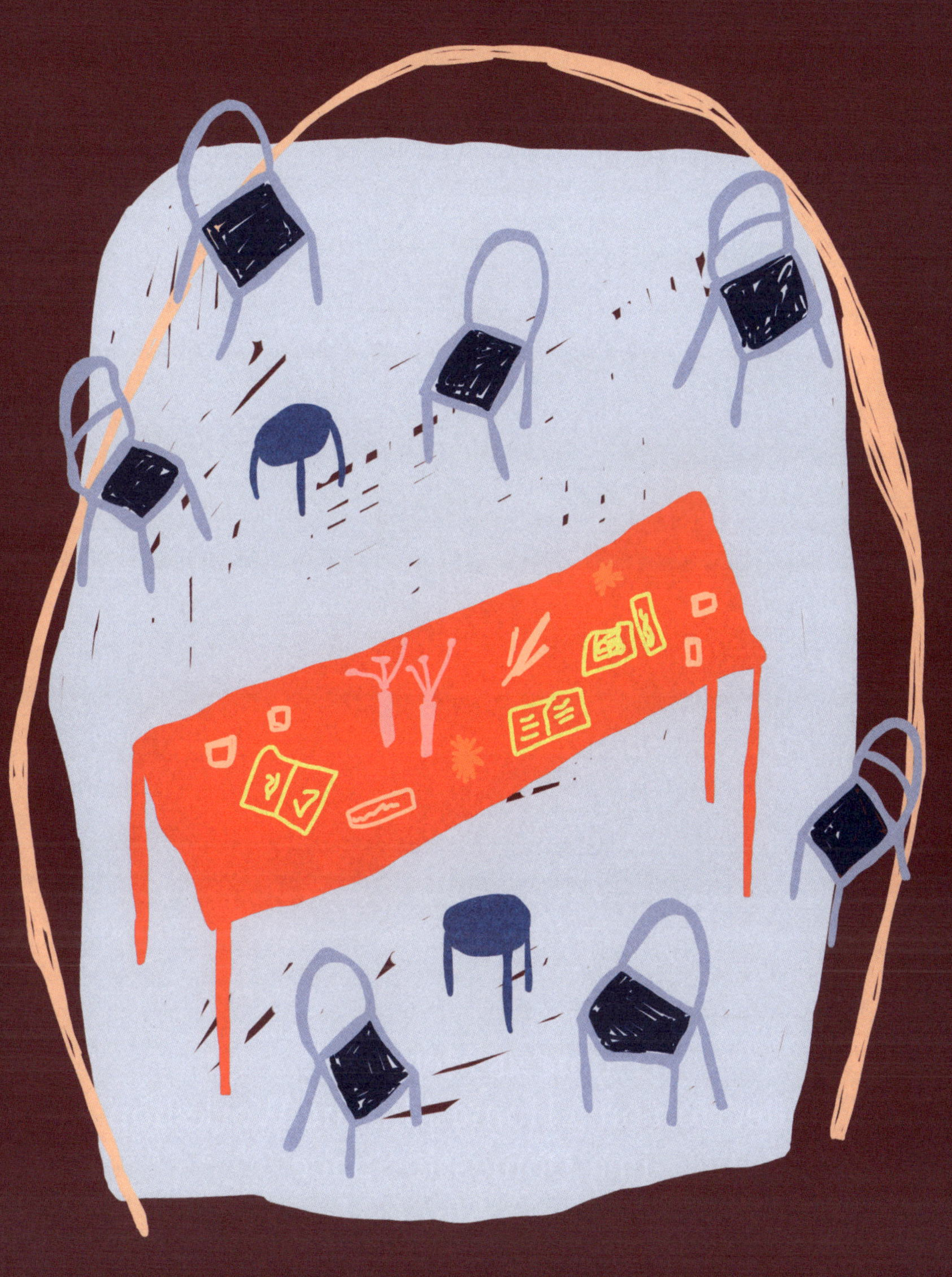

Home as Method:[58]
Reflection on a Home-Making Workshop in a Domestic Space

Kevin Shu LAI

This entry was written in October 2023 as a reflection on the trials and tribulations in hosting a home-making workshop earlier in that same year. Two years later I am now revising this text in Amsterdam, some days after I was abruptly evicted by my landlord from my apartment. It is difficult to read one's work. This text is juvenile. The lack of academic rigor is blatant. I wish not to publish this. Or, the entire text needs to be shredded down and rebuilt from ground-zero. But this text is perhaps most valuable for its freshness – a field note quickly scribbled down. I could not have written the same now. His rumination was a product of his uneasiness with belonging in the new worlds he found himself in, and an attempt to orient in the shifting landscape of architectural education in his sixth year in the discipline. In this release, I decide to leave the edits to the original text at the minimum to present the account raw.[59] *With that, we observe the observer...*

Dreispitz is a residential neighborhood in Schwamendingen, adjacent to Oerlikon in the north of Zurich. In Dreispitz, there are four-hundred-fifty-seven affordable residential units in two-hundred-twenty-three single-family and twenty-three multi-family houses, the majority of which can be dated back to the 1940s. The terrace houses are laid in a clear orientation to the sun, sitting in a luscious green of private gardens. Hedges are tall and flank the narrow paths that are just wide enough for a car. A cyclist would have to carefully negotiate space with a pedestrian. From Oerlikon station I arrive at the northern edge by bus. Over a flight of steps I step into the neighborhood. On the ground are kitchens and toilets. Domestic life billows through the ceramic grilles. I check my phone for the address Michael sent me. He and Qianer are my hosts for the next two weeks. Michael greets me at the door and shows me inside. I feel comforted to see this old friend from Hong Kong. It is a dewy morning. We walk towards the garden. And there I see over the horizon - Dreispitz would soon be demolished and redeveloped into a densified quarter of new housing units. The residents of Dreispitz are required to

58
This title is inspired by: Yiu-Wai Chu, ed., *Hong Kong Culture and Society in the New Millennium*, vol. 4, The Humanities in Asia (Singapore: Springer, 2017).
This book, which approaches the discipline from a methodological perspective, advocates for a critical position on Hong Kong studies within the framework of post-colonialism. It remains a dear reference to me as I navigate the academic world in Europe as a mobile body from Hong Kong.

59
[RE] Original footnotes are kept per se. Footnotes added in the 2025 revision are marked with *[RE]*

move out by the end of 2023. Construction has already begun on the south-east tangent where the municipality has proceeded full-force ahead with an Ueberlandpark project elevating a pedestrian green corridor over a busy vehicular highway. This impending fate of Dreispitz is right here. We are just feet away from bulldozers in the backyard. Pepe, our free-spirited cat, is kept from wandering out during construction. In the late hours when everything goes quiet, a thought churns the stomach: *Can we talk about home, at home?* [60]

60
[RE] In retrospect, the question can benefit from better framed in a critical framework relating property, ownership, and family organization: How can social relations be underscored in the neighborhood of Dreispitz in the face of its demolition?

61
The workshop was part of a series exploring alternative learning modes, organized by *Unmasking Space*. A group of sixteen students participated in the eleven available seminars, each offering a unique lens and setting, and together, they explored alternative approaches to learning architecture.
The syllabus of the credit-bearing elective organized by *Unmasking Space*, a student-led course at ETH Zurich, is available at: https://unmasking.space/Syllabus

62
[RE] Katherine is a friend from Hong Kong. She is an architect based in London. 60

Figure 1
The kitchen wall at Dreispitz with messages left behind by participant-guests as final farewell, 2023. Photo Credits and Copyright: Kevin Shu LAI.

This sets the backdrop for the two home-making sessions with *Unmasking Space* that took place in April 2023.[61] Katherine[62] and I were invited to submit a workshop plan related to their pedagogical agenda, to rethink and reflect on the forms and modes of knowledge production in architectural institutions. Our conversation began

They asked me to design a house,

in London, in the summer of 2022 in the midst of one of the worst heatwaves in Europe. There I was interviewing recent arrivals from Hong Kong to study the urban significance of the late mass migration. Katherine hosted me in London for a week. Then I left for Berlin. There in Südkreuz, I wrote the workshop proposal from my summer sublet, submerged in the domestic life of another person I did not know.

Figure 2
Close-up on auto-ethnographies by participant-guests, 2023. Photo Credits and Copyright: Kevin Shu LAI.

We proposed the initial idea of foregrounding "home" as a site of learning, or better, a situation of learning. During the workshop we aimed to develop tools with the participants to unmask their own homes through an auto-ethnographic gaze, while encouraging them to own up to their partial vision[63] as designer-inhabitants of their own space. As such, the workshop represented an attempt to create an intimate space that acknowledges the subjectivities of each designer-inhabitant, where stories on the tangents of migration, displacement,[64] domesticity, belonging, identity, and more can be discussed in the framework of an education module. We wanted to question the translation of the act of home-making as an act of place-making, particularly for those disempowered in effecting changes in their environments due to structural difficulty over their identity, gender, economic status, and residence rights. Understanding identity as a repetition of performative enactments, we intended the workshop to serve as a translation exercise. The workshop was structured in two parts: first, exploration on ways of making home in a domestic setting, and second, a translation practice of home-making in an institutional space.

63
The concept of "partial vision" is borrowed from: Donna Haraway, 'Situated Knowledges: The Science Question in Feminism and the Privilege of Partial Perspective', *Feminist Studies* 14, no. 3 (1988): 575–99.

64
[RE] It becomes apparent to me now the attempt then to discuss "displacement" within the circle of students in ETHZ, TU Delft, and AA represents naivety among the academic elites, and violence at worst, towards real worlds, despite our best effort to be otherwise.

Kevin asked them to design a home

Learning from one's home should not be a foreign idea after the global pandemic. Our domestic space is switched on when the online chatroom opens, either carefully curated in the background or aggressively blurred out. But that is not the story we are interested in. We are interested in the pedagogical value in learning from one's private home: *What is the methodological value of a domestic space for alternative learning outside of its thematic relevance to domesticity?* Think of *House X* by the Boyarsky family in relation to the Architectural Association in Bedford Square.[65] We want to recall the actual experience of the home-making workshop to reflect on what worked and what not.

Michael and Qianer are dear friends of mine. Together with Airas and Pepe they share the three-storey in Dreispitz, with a living room conjoined with a kitchen on the ground and two bedrooms upstairs. Plus an attic, a garden, and a basement. Michael and Qianer are among the organizers of *Unmasking Space*. Dreispitz was in the limbo of anticipating a new redevelopment. That means lower rent and therefore lower threshold. This was the reason they managed to afford their tenancy in the first place. The anticipated displacement from Dreispitz introduced a reality to the workshop: How do we navigate our sense of belonging in transit? As a guest from the Netherlands, I was offered to stay at the same house during my time in Zurich. A form of domestic hospitality was at play. I connected with old friends over their delicious Cantonese cooking and encountered new faces in other intimate dinners in the garden. Michael offered his studio space in the basement as my private bedroom. In the mornings I was joined by Qianer at the table as we planned out the final details of the upcoming workshop. Some nights Airas was cooking with us in the kitchen when Pepe just returned from his daily walk. I was the invited guest. The house was a space of hospitality and that same hospitality was extended out in the first home-making session.

Three texts were prepared for a collective reading on that day.[66] They were selected for their distance in their time of writing and their theoretical contrasts on the notion of "home." Printed in open spreads in A0 posters, the page sequence dissolved and a landscape across the sheet emerged. Then the house was open. The participant-guests started arriving. Along with Qianer and Michael I greeted them as the host of the space. The participant-guests were

They asked me to design a house,

65
See Nicholas Boyarsky, "House X", in *Activism at Home: Architects Dwelling between Politics, Aesthetics and Resistance*, ed. Isabelle Doucet and Janina Gosseye (Berlin: Jovis, 2021), 159–70.

66
The three selected texts are: Guillermo Lopez and Anna Puigjaner, "Everyday Life in the Diffuse House", in *Everyday Matters: Contemporary Approaches to Architecture*, ed. Vanessa Grossman and Ciro Miguel (Berlin: Ruby Press, 2021), 34-49; Georges Perec, *Species of Spaces and Other Pieces* (London: Penguin Books, 1997), 24–25, 26–39; Donna Haraway, "Situated Knowledges: The Science Question in Feminism and the Privilege of Partial Perspective", *Feminist Studies* 14, no. 3 (1988): 575–99.

introduced through the hallway into the living room. They either settled into their own corners on the couch, next to the houseplants, in the kitchen, or ended up in the garden for extra sun. As the house started to fill up, people would brush their shoulders against the tight hallway. Conversations overlapped and swoll up into a cacophony. The critical mass. The house was charged with a shared intimacy cushioned by music in the background. The architectural sequence of the house provided corners and thresholds for small talks which stand in contrast to the "big talks" in academic language. There was no obvious orientation in this learning space; that is to say, any orientation could be possible afforded by different spatial dispositions. We were reading on a wall lit by the south window, on the dinner table, and in the garden to enjoy the clear sky after a week of rain. We circled and highlighted the texts in each of our chosen colors. The intimacy allowed for a non-hierarchical space of learning together, in the same fashion that Katherine and I positioned ourselves as hosts who were also participants. I was both the guest and the host. In retrospect, maybe this intimacy speaks of an alternative pedagogy, that is not confined to a room but to a multitude of rooms, i.e. a house. And a house is not comparable to a campus. Because scale matters. The small house in Dreispitz, sequenced in tight hallways and doors to rooms, presents a domestic scenography where architecture could be learnt.

But could it be more than a scenography?

That was the question that arose during the planning of the second session. It was designed to take place in the institutional space of ETHZ, where participants would bring over their methods of home-making unmasked at individual homes and apply them to make a "home" in the institute. We had passionate discussions among ourselves about whether this translation back into the school environment was significant enough to the workshop's success at the cost of foregoing the intimacy in our domestic space. The translation exercise was intended to experiment with ways of constructing a sense of belonging in another space, i.e. a place-making exercise. Establishing a stark spatial contrast between the two sessions would be ideal to stretch the limit of this translation. It was a good intention, but we unanimously agreed it was misguided. In the first session we explored the formal qualities of home as a learning space that is intimate and non-hierarchical. Revisiting a space can reinforce that initial encounter. Continuity should be valued over contrast.

While we acknowledged the power of theatrics, opening a discussion about home-making in a domestic setting goes beyond staging. The scenography should remain, but we, as hosts and participants, should be more than just a watchful audience. We should engage with the house using our bodies with its idiosyncrasies and contradictions while experiencing the reality of its impending demolition. It was not a "site visit" to Dreispitz as we conventionally understand in our architectural education. We were not meant to extract anything from the "site." Ultimately, the workshop was meant to bring the participants' domestic subjectivities into dialogue with that of Dreispitz. As such, the second session decidedly stayed at Dreispitz.

Figure *3*
Close-up on auto-ethnographies by participant-guests, 2023. Photo Credits and Copyright: Kevin Shu LAI.

The house was open. Our participant-guests started arriving. We greeted them in a familiar hospitality, only now with deeper trust. Music started playing. Someone remarked jokingly that it was turning into a house exhibition. Everyone was encouraged to find a sweet spot to display their findings over the week. One found the door hinge, another found the shower tub, another found the kitchen hatch door to the living room, someone else found the bulkhead at the top of the staircase, another found the wall skirting around the living room, and another found the floor. They brought their auto-ethnographies from their own homes into encountering each other in Dreispitz. "I'm so glad we decided to stay here," Katherine

They asked me to design a house,

said with relief over Zoom from London as she witnessed the whole joyous bustle. Indeed a good decision. The house, made into a loving home by Qianer, Michael, Airas, and Pepe, generously provided the session with an intimate and safe space where everyone could feel comfortable sharing their personal stories. This intimacy would not be impossible but difficult in the institutional spaces where we have been taught architecture. Here our act of exhibiting ways of home-making has become an act of *making home* in Dreispitz.

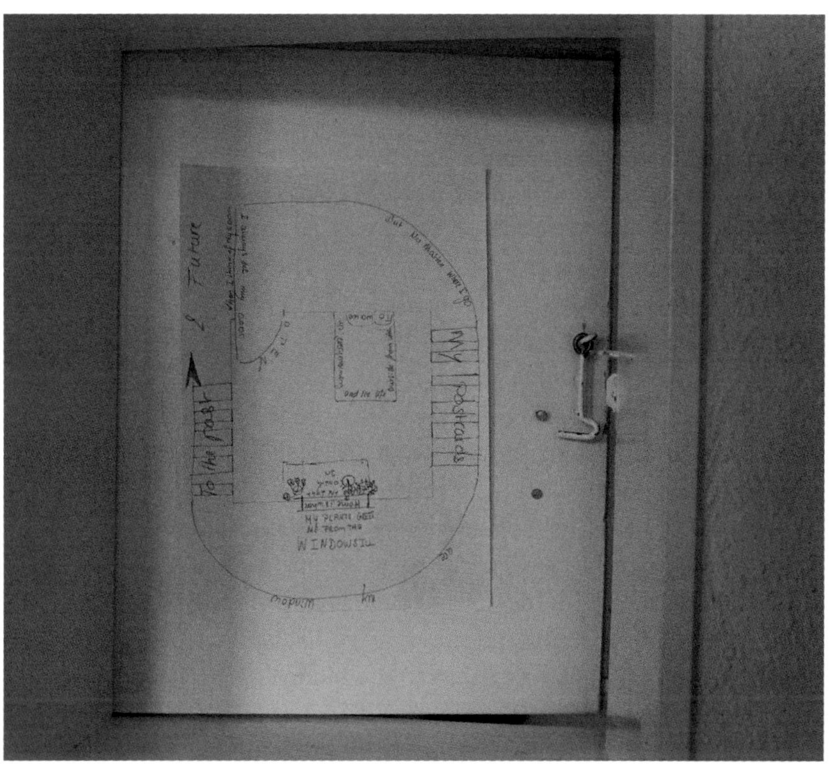

Figure 4
Close-up on auto-ethnographies by participant-guests, 2023. Photo Credits and Copyright: Kevin Shu LAI.

In these two sessions, the dozen of us, students from ETHZ and abroad, collectively transformed the architecture of a house into a home. As such, learning became an exercise of relating to other bodies and other stories. Here our bodies were more relaxed. Our jaws softened around the language we used. The clinical jargons dissolved. We became more accommodating to "I dunno's" and "maybe's." Maybe this is the generosity we are missing in our architectural learning. We can hesitate. We can be unsure of our work. We can reveal ourselves from behind the mask of scientific expertise. If "home" can be a method, it could possibly be a method of being aware of one's situatedness and subjectivity in discussing architecture. Intimacy at home reshuffles the power hierarchy of architectural learning. We begin to think this intimacy can be designed through the act of hospitality. Hospitality can be more than a social etiquette. Hospitality is about power and the extension of power. Hospitality delineates the hosts and the guests. Yet, my experience at Dreispitz proposed a third position: kins. I was a guest in their everyday life in the house as much as I was a host for the workshop. It is no coincidence that advocating for home-as-method alludes to questions of kinship raised in queer theories. Learning architecture involves finding relationships. The enthusiasm over theories on relationality in the field of architecture now not only reorients discourse in schools where the discipline can no longer be considered insular. It also mandates our reflection on our ways of learning architecture. The language of kinship has been instrumentalized to define posthuman and multispecies terms. My hypothesis is that an alternative mode of learning can be argued using the same language. The home at Dreispitz was the necessary form to present a new social imaginary of hosts and guests: We are making kins.

As I am writing this reflection in my bedroom in Delft, I cannot help but wonder: *All theories aside, how is this home-making workshop at Dreispitz a valuable reference to others?* I don't know. I cannot claim that this format should be replicated in the form of pastiche for any subjects of architectural education, nor can I argue for a theorization of "home" as a pedagogical framework. But here I am reminded of the impending reality of Dreispitz. It will be gone months from now. As I now listen to the recording of our last session, I heard myself saying: "...with demolition inches away, our workshop here in Dreispitz serves not only as an educational module but also as a real political act of resistance." It was a privilege and a pleasure to collaborate with *Unmasking Space* along with Katherine on thinking of a new mode of decentralized knowledge production. There is a political agency embedded in the initiative that, once again, in a gesture of hospitality, was extended to us as individuals, hosts, and participants alike. I am reminded of other parts of the world where learning in public can be censored and muted. A domestic space is indeed one of the last safe havens for discussing freely and openly. Maybe a decentralized way of learning has already been practiced at individual homes. Home has always been our method.

**This article was first submitted in October 2023, and subsequently revised in February 2025.*

They asked me to design a house,

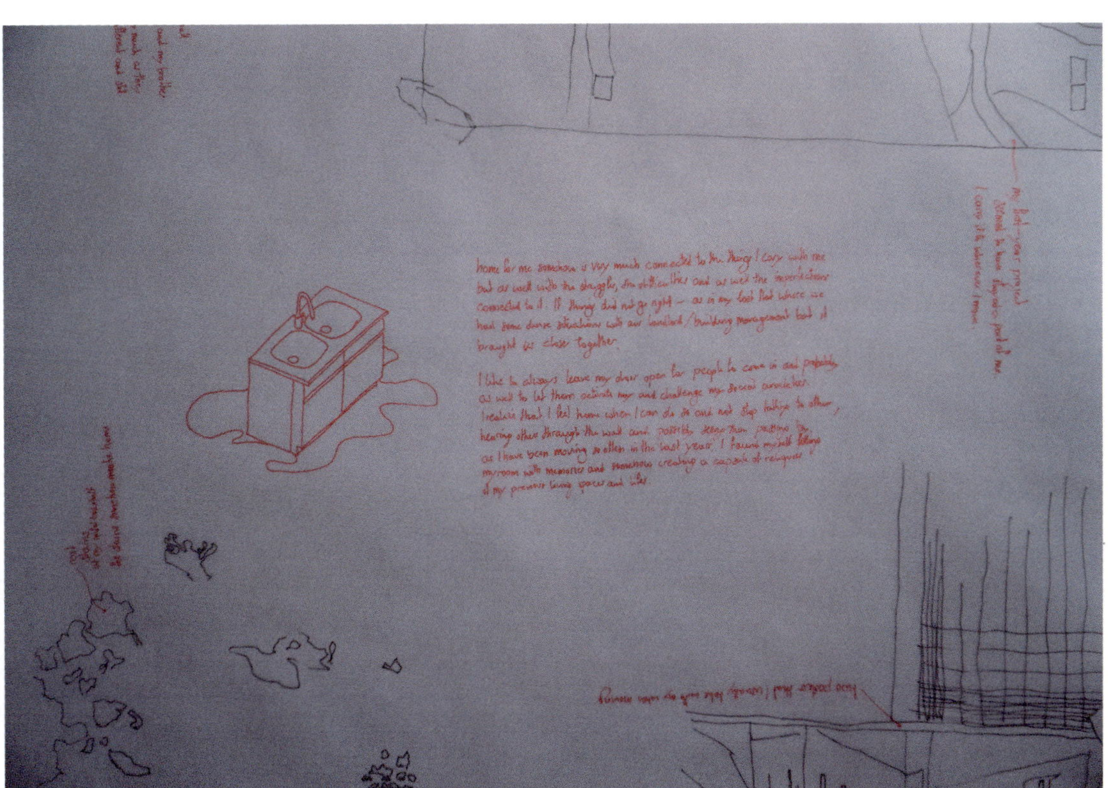

Figure *5*
Close-up on auto-ethnographies by participant-guests, 2023. Photo Credits and Copyright: Kevin Shu LAI.

Kevin asked them to design a home

KEVIN SHU LAI (he/him) is a researcher based in Amsterdam and Hong Kong. He is trained as an architect. His research interests lie at the intersection of urban political ecology scholarship and post-colonial historiography.

They asked me to design a house,

Living Architecture: Empathy as a Building Practice

Conversation with la-di-da

UNDER THE CARPET

ILARIA AND GEORGINA As architects, how did you initiate your practice in affordable house design? And as educators, how do you approach this topic in an educational environment?

LAURA We approach the word "empathy" both in designing a house and in considering the materials used. In teaching, talking with the undergraduates about designing a house, we emphasize understanding materials in relation to their development, mining impact, and life cycle. We empathize with the broader context rather than solely pursuing form, aiming to intervene in the material life cycle to improve conditions for builders, growers and the environment.

DIEDERIK We emphasize ergonomics, like cutting boards into smaller pieces to enhance builders' comfort during facade work. While architecture is often discussed in terms of shape, we don't often talk about it as a performance. I think of the material almost as a stakeholder. Anyway, to give a bit of context, we graduated after the 2008 crisis, so there was not much that was being built.

LAURA We met at a design studio for wood at the Architecture department in Delft. All the other courses were about concrete, steel, and massive housing projects. I went to Finland to learn more about wood construction and then we collaborated on a pilot studio called Urban Emergencies, for redeveloping housing after natural disasters. We went to Bangladesh together for three months and started studying the domestic phenomenon from a planning point of view.

DIEDERIK After World War II, the baby boom brought about the idea that domestic life was synonymous with owning a house. Today, with rising prices, owning a house has become increasingly difficult. By building at an ecological and affordable level, architecture can serve as a tool to support people. In many ways, the simple availability of housing is the first step toward true domesticity. Our aim has been to give the middle and lower-middle class the opportunity to afford a home.

LAURA Do you have the game we made for the design process?

DIEDERIK (showing the game): This is what we used for the conversations with the clients. It's also an example of how the dimension becomes the consequence of the material. You have modules that are set and you build around those.

LAURA We research how to respect and minimize material use. We don't work with massive wood construction. We completed four projects, each smaller than the last: the first was 300 sqm, followed by 150 sqm, 100 sqm, and finally, 50 sqm. We progressively took over the responsibility of the construction. In the Netherlands you work with the contractor, who hires the subcontractor and takes full responsibility for the project. We more and more took over that role. In a way, we are also taking over the developer role which allows us to build much more affordably. Surely you enter a sort of gray zone as an architect, since you are accountable for any kind of miscommunications.

DIEDERIK We have a very domestic architecture office. This is our office but also our home and people sometimes think that's unprofessional. Like, "domestic" would mean unprofessional. But we think this is a very interesting way of working as we can also be personal with the clients. I recently had a discussion at the didactic course at the Royal Academy of Art (KABK) regarding their ambitions to teach students to become professionals, a wording that recalls an economic business system. Not being professional is somehow what we want to achieve as well; to be able to have a personal relationship with people. Ultimately, this is not a transaction.

GEORGINA In discussions with users, how do you navigate the process of presenting and convincing them that your idea is more beneficial for their needs?

DIEDERIK I don't think it is a matter of convincing. In design, the cheapest thing you can do is change your behavior.

ILARIA Do you think that when your clients understand this system (referring to the module game), they also approach your question/answer differently, more in line with what you'd suggest?

DIEDERIK That's also what we thought, but I don't think it actually works that well. Maybe it is not the right tool yet. We have to figure it out.

LAURA This is also the result of these four projects. If we want to scale up, we have to reconsider some things.

DIEDERIK I find the distinction between the perception of a house and the architecture of domesticity fascinating. Many people envision 'the dream house,' but this mindset is often unproductive as anything you design risks shattering their illusion. Instead, you can engage meaningfully with the idea of the domestic environment by moving beyond the concept of a dream house and focusing on personal habits and needs.

The first house we designed was for my parents, which was both awkward and interesting, as it allowed me to see them from a new perspective. We had this funny moment when my father, who is more of an evening person, came to bed late and woke up my mum, who is a morning person. How do we solve that? We designed a bedroom with individual corridors and wardrobes leading to a shared swinging door. My father's side faced west, and my mother's side faced east, with the bed placed at the intersection of these axes. These to me are the sort of simple domestic specificities that can positively transform how we live, even if they don't fit the traditional notion of a dream house.

LAURA We try to break the obsession of form out of the system. Form is and becomes, but it is not the status quo. People are still proud of how an architecture/building/facade looks from the outside. That's not the point at all; you should design from the inside out.

Figure 1–4
(not) bedroom, showing symmetry, 2015.
Photo Credits and Copyright: Peter Tijhuis.

They asked me to design a house,

la-di-da asked them to design a home

ILARIA ⸙ Can you show us something you are working on at the moment?

LAURA ⸙ This is the palette we developed with wood insulation. We always joke about it as we built it in wood, but from the outside it looks like concrete because of the cement coat for the fire regulation. We are now in touch with a company to see if we can make a bio-based alternative to that cement coat.

DIEDERIK ⸙ We are also developing a proposal for foundation poles. The top part is usually in concrete, but I think we need to consider our limitations as individuals and avoid constructing everything as if it has to last for eternity.
For my PhD research I look at prehistoric farms. Archeologists often discover wood removed from the building and applied elsewhere as it was still a resource. You build a house for a person, and then when that person dies, the family dismantles it and builds their own. I find this question of the forever lasting of architecture very bizarre.

GEORGINA ⸙ It's the first time that I hear something like that from an architect, as we have often been taught that, as architects, we have to leave a mark.

LAURA ⸙ We went back to Diederik's parents' house and we documented the decay and the use. The book *Material Cultures: Material Reform* is a great inspiration for us. The authors also wrote an introductory article in *NOOK magazine (BNI)* about the idea of aesthetics, considering how things smell and building with healthy materials.

DIEDERIK ⸙ or me, this is joy. You have something that can capture life. It tells a story. Domesticity is a story to share.

LAURA ⸙ Of course, you don't want active rooting, but you can think whether it can be more acceptable or not. Sometimes we also teach at the Academy of Architecture in Amsterdam. We observe the need to challenge people's conditioning in building culture. Students often struggle to convey the value of life traces to clients, especially in the Dutch context, where there is even an obsession with removing grass between tiles.

GEORGINA ⸙ In Mediterranean culture, we have the exact opposite. The house has to be perfect from the inside. For me, this is a combination of different cultural elements that are reflected in the house.

DIEDERIK ⸙ I think it's interesting that we don't need to have a solution. But for us, it has been mentally relaxing to tackle things from a different perspective.

LAURA ⸙ When we give lectures, we also like to share the "beautiful accidents" that have occurred because this is part of what architecture is about – allowing others to learn. And that comes with the idea of a more shared responsibility.

DIEDERIK ⸙ We need more of that; understanding the shared responsibility. It's much more fair than having your own contractor make a lot of money if nothing goes wrong. We have to talk about that, and the same goes for the material.

ILARIA ⸙ Do you want to teach because

They asked me to design a house,

this needs to be shared and is not yet on everyone's agenda?

LAURA ⁓ Yes. There are a lot of urgent things of course; decolonization, social injustice, inclusivity, biodiversity. But this is our focus. In the bachelor's program we changed our entire curriculum so the students work with understanding waste flows, for example.

DIEDERIK ⁓ In affordable building education, the traditional studio structure may not provide sufficient impact. There's a need to consider a teaching curriculum that extends beyond a single studio. You would spend a whole education on these kinds of topics. My biggest inspiration for that is Rural Studio in Alabama. Instead of focusing on immediate solutions, this approach sees each student's contribution as part of a cumulative process. I believe implementing a similar initiative in the Netherlands would be beneficial, and would require a long-term educational system rather than short-term competitions. It underscores the idea that knowledge is an ongoing maintenance process, not a one-time achievement.

LAURA ⁓ USP – Unique Selling Point; I learned this word yesterday. Society is overly concerned with that: worried about having to find the perfect solution, instead of making it collectively and open source.

DIEDERIK ⁓ One of the worst things someone could say to us is that we've found an interesting niche, as it implies this work reflects our personal ideal. What we're trying to convey is that this isn't about us, it's about addressing something that needs to happen on a societal level. We do this work not for ourselves but because it's essential for societal progress.

Figure 5–8
Aged materials. Originally for NOOK magazine, 2023.
Photo Credits and Copyright: Jeannette Slütter.

They asked me to design a house,

la-di-da asked them to design a home

LA-DI-DA, Laura van Santen and Diederik de Koning share the design and architecture studio la-di-da (2015, The Hague).
They are driven by curiosity and an eagerness to understand the entire construction process from raw material to product. As every line on paper has an ecological and social impact elsewhere on the planet, they feel that architects need to take full responsibility for designs they make. In collaboration with various workshops, they conduct material experiments to develop new architectural products. They share this knowledge at several academies of design and architecture around the Netherlands, and apply their knowledge in commissioned projects.

They asked me to design a house,

A Single Woman's Home

Michele Rinaldi

UNDER THE CARPET

In the words of the painter and journalist Rosa Menni Giolli, “The woman, even more than the man, loves the home.” This sentence, published in the article ‘La Casa Di Una Donna Sola’ (‘A single woman’s home’) in 1933 for the Italian women’s magazine *Eva*,[67] captures a truth that resonates through the tumultuous first half of the 20th century. In an era marked by profound changes and the promise of modernization, the role of women, particularly single women, within the evolving concept of home, is nothing short of complex. While the modernization of homes mirrored societal shifts, including urban nomadism and singlehood, it is essential to ask: What stories lie beneath the title of Giolli’s article? What has history overlooked? Was the home really a sanctuary for women in Italy during this transformative period, especially for those who were single?

Singlehood, a result of the Industrial Revolution and the rise of urbanization, marked a profound shift in societal dynamics during the late 19th and early 20th centuries.[68] This transformation gave birth to a new array of housing solutions, including dormitories, boarding houses, and minimal dwellings. This trend transcended national boundaries and had a global impact, with initial strongholds in the United States and the United Kingdom. In particular, the Rowton Houses in the UK, which emerged in the late 19th century, paved the way for other innovative housing projects in continental Europe. Italy eagerly absorbed this concept. In fact, Milan became the site of a ground-breaking initiative: the Albergo Popolare in 1901. It was the first of its kind outside the UK and sought to provide decent and contemporary accommodations for single men arriving in the bustling city for business or work.[69] During the 1920s, however, the housing model evolved to reflect the modernization and lifestyle changes of the time. It was a time when architects, designers, and visionaries showcased novel designs specifically tailored to single individuals. This transformation, epitomized in the German housing exhibitions organized by the Deutscher Werkbund and the CIAM, marked a profound shift in the definition of minimal housing.[70]

67
Rosa Giolli Menni, "La Casa Di Una Donna Sola", *Eva* 1, no. 8 (April 1933).

68
Ariadne Schmidt, Isabelle Devos, and Bruno Blondé, "Single and the City: Men and Women Alone in North-Western European Towns since the Late Middle Ages", in *Single Life and the City 1200–1900*, ed. Julie De Groot, Isabelle Devos, and Ariadne Schmidt (London: Palgrave Macmillan, 2015), 1-24.

69
Gianfranco Pugni, *C'era Una Volta l'albergo. La Vicenda Dell'Albergo Popolare Di Milano* (CRAL Ospedale S. Paolo, 2001).

70
Markus Eisen, *Vom Ledigenheim zum Boardinghouse: Bautypologie und Gesellschaftstheorie bis zum Ende der Weimarer Republik* (Berlin: Gebr. Mann Verlag, 2012).

Although Italy was a part of this discourse, its trajectory differed. The Albergo Popolare in Milan remained a solitary architectural gem in the early 20th century, serving as a testament to the country's changing political and cultural landscape.

The rise of fascism in Italy during the 1930s had a profound impact on housing initiatives. This era saw housing initiatives wielded as tools of complex propaganda, with housing at the very core of this narrative. During that time, minimal housing concepts inspired by architectural trends in Germany gained traction in Italy. Notably, the Milan Triennials played a central role in showcasing these architectural experiments. While they timidly displayed prototypes of houses designed for single men, outside of these exhibitions, architects sought to introduce housing models to accommodate the needs of single people, though predominantly men. However, the rhetoric of increased households and birth rates often stymied these initiatives.

Figure 1
Antonietta (Sophia Loren) in a scene from *A Special Day (Una giornata particolare)*, directed by Ettore Scola, 1977. Screenshot from the film.
Source: Wikimedia Commons.

During this tumultuous period, Rosa Menni Giolli emerged as a passionate voice against the status quo. In a commendable show of resilience and advocacy, she voiced concerns about the conditions endured by single women. It's important to remember that attempts to provide housing for single working women in Italian cities had early beginnings. Luigi Buffoli, the visionary behind the Albergo Popolare in Milan, recognized the need for accommodation for women, sparking the concept of a women's hotel.[71] Unfortunately, this ambitious project never saw the light of day. During the twenty-year rule of fascism, the plight of single women worsened. The state

71
'In Memoriam. Luigi Buffoli' (Stabilimento Tipografico dell'Unione Cooperativa – Milano, 1911).

They asked me to design a house,

effectively barred unmarried women from the housing market. However, dissent simmered beneath the surface, and Rosa Menni Giolli's voice became an impassioned dissonant note.

Rosa Menni Giolli was born in Milan in 1889 into a wealthy bourgeoisie family of progressive ideas, which allowed her to encounter numerous personalities from the worlds of culture, art, and entertainment. She studied at the Royal Academy of Fine Arts in Brera and opened her own atelier in Milan after graduating. While initially a painter, she gradually shifted towards applied decorative art. In 1921, she established her own workshop and production line *Le stoffe della Rosa*. Throughout the 1920s, she achieved great success in exhibitions and won prestigious prizes. Menni Giolli collaborated with renowned figures in the fashion and design industry, such as Gio Ponti. However, with the rise of the fascist regime, Menni Giolli and her husband faced difficulties as anti-fascist activists. After being persecuted by the regime and her husband's death in a concentration camp in the post-war period, she continued her work as a translator until her death in 1975.

Figure 2
Photographic portrait of Rosa Menni Giolli, from *Le mie stoffe*, Milano, Galleria Pesaro, 1923. Source: Wikimedia Commons. Copyright: public domain.

In the 1930s, she began contributing to architecture magazines like *Domus* and *Casabella*, eventually venturing into publishing with the women's magazine *Eva*. In her 1933 article, 'La Casa Di Una Donna Sola' ('A single woman's home'), she made a resounding call for modern housing standards, American-inspired and custom-made for single women. She criticized the dependency of women on their husbands for access to public housing, highlighting the ordeal of obtaining affordable, comfortable, and modern homes.[72]

The 1930s witnessed women's magazines evolving into platforms for innovative ideas about small apartment design and multi-functional furniture. Architectural projects, both from established and emerging architects, were showcased. Beneath the alluring facade of domestic modernity, the home transformed into a realm of adversity for women, particularly those who were denied the chance of education and economic emancipation. Instead of being a place of belonging, it often became a site of oppression and an environment where survival was compelled, contrary to the portrayal by the regime and women's publications. An exquisite portrait of this condition is represented by Ettore Scola's masterful 1977 film *A Special Day*, in which Antonietta, played by Sophia Loren, embodies the dreams and repressions of the 1930s Italian housewife.[73]

While this may appear as a distant and antiquated chapter in Italy's historical narrative, its reverberations echo across the tapestry of our contemporary world, resonating on a global scale. It serves as a poignant reminder of the enduring marginalization faced by various minority groups today – whether due to factors of ethnicity, religion, sexual orientation, or disability – when it comes to the fundamental right of securing affordable housing in the bustling heart of urban life. In our modern era, single individuals are emerging as the swiftest-growing social cohort, yet the attainment of housing remains an elusive privilege.[74] This challenge is further compounded for those who belong to marginalized groups, echoing the struggles of women in 20th-century Italy.

Moreover, within the folds of this long-forgotten chapter, closely intertwined with Rosa Menni Giolli's article, lies an eloquent testament to the transformative potential of publishing as a critical practice. It beautifully underscores how, in retrospect, media publications, even when filtered through official narratives, wield

72
Giolli Menni, "La Casa Di Una Donna Sola".

73
Ettore Scola, *Una Giornata Particolare* (1977).

74
Schmidt, Devos, and Blondé, "Single and the City".

They asked me to design a house,

a profound influence in shaping our understanding of history and society. Revisiting and reinterpreting historical sources, as such, emerges as an act of profound inclusion.

The quest for equitable housing endures, echoing through the annals of time and underscoring the tremendous potential for advocacy, media, and design to champion the cause of marginalized individuals. Rosa Menni Giolli's call for modernization, championing women's rights to housing, remains a testament to the power of design as a vehicle for equality and liberation within the intimate confines of the domestic sphere. It stands as a powerful reminder of the enduring role of the home, not merely as a physical shelter but as a symbol of personal emancipation and the embodiment of freedom.

EVA

10

La casa di una donna sola

ROSA GIOLLI MENNI

CUCINA MODERNA

CORALLINA

Figure 3
Page extract from Rosa Menni Giolli, "La Casa di Una Donna Sola," Eva 1, no. 1 (15 April 1933): 10. Copyright: not definitively determined.

MICHELE RINALDI is a PhD student in History of Architecture at Politecnico di Torino, Italy, and KU Leuven, Belgium.
His research traverses the history of housing, exploring various perspectives and scales from domesticity to the domestic interior, employing an interdisciplinary approach. Michele holds a degree in Architecture from the University of Bologna, Italy, and brings a background in professional practice to his academic pursuits.
He has previously worked as an architect in Berlin and participated in academic programmes centred on curating architecture exhibitions and archives, offered by the AA School of Architecture in London and the MAXXI in Rome.

They asked me to design a house,

Staged Intimacies and the Labor of Home
Conversation with Nicholas Korody

UNDER THE CARPET

ILARIA AND GEORGINA How did your research on domesticity start?

NICHOLAS It's difficult to pinpoint where my interest in domesticity began. Domesticity is the spatial environment we are most familiar with – it's the one we actively shape and intervene in. What fascinated me was the lack of attention given to interiors within academic discourse. It has been largely overlooked by Western critical thought, not just within architectural schools, but also by sociologists and philosophers. I remember when I applied to university: I asked my mom to check my application letter, and she would mark the words "interior decoration" every time I wrote them. I was interested in the everyday practice of decorating, the non-professional decorating process carried out by everyone. But this is traditionally done by women, mothers, and wives. My mum would erase the word "decoration" and put "design" instead. This already reflects the hierarchy embedded in how we define what makes an interior significant, as well as the value we assign to the act of shaping it. It's dramatic if you think about the scale of what non-professional decoration is. Economically alone, it is part of the global market. That was what interested me, but also what videotelephony does to the spatial environment, enabling new forms of work, sex work, and consumption of media. It seems to me that the idea of the house as we traditionally think of it, was never true to begin with. We have this image of the house as a static environment that doesn't change. However, the house is the architectural space that is the most transformed by social and economic transformation.

ILARIA How do you think concepts of intimacy and its opposite are applied in the architectural domesticity sphere?

NICHOLAS Intimacy is a key theme in my work. For example, if you look at the sex industry, you will notice the boom of porn in the 70s and 80s. Then, with the new forms of e-sex work and online sex cam, you see spaces that used to host such businesses redecorated to look like a domestic bedroom. This adaptation stems from the vulnerability of the home, protecting against online threats and accommodating workers with disapproving families. Many cam workers opt for expensive studios that mimic bedrooms, leveraging the erotic capital attached to personality.
If you ask anyone who works in the sex industry, either traditionally or virtually, so much of the work is meant to establish a sense of intimacy. A design strategy set by cam workers is to work in a space that looks like a bedroom because the consumer has the urge to have easier access to the inhabitant. There is a normative belief that the home is a representation of the person who inhabits it. Decorating is a form of self-expression that also conceals a significant amount of work and economic pressure in determining how and why people decorate. It's an odd belief, if you think that most houses look the same.
In the U.S., there's the Child Protection Unit, which can visit your home, and if they deem it's not "domestic enough," they have the authority to remove your

Nicholas asked them to design a home

children. Similarly, when selling a house, home staging often involves stripping away personal signifiers, under the belief that buyers should be able to project themselves into the space, like a blank canvas or a theatrical set for livability. There's a striking case in the U.S. where a Black woman discovered that her house was appraised far lower than her neighbors' homes. After removing all signs of her Black identity and having a white friend show the house to a different appraiser, the value increased dramatically. This illustrates how the political dimensions of domesticity are often overlooked. It's fascinating to question what intimacy truly means and how it's altered when constantly exposed by the media.

GEORGINA In a recent project, I aimed to bridge the gap between my grandma's house and my personal intimacy in that space, recognizing that elements tied to intimacy align with a feminist perspective. Whereas, aspects less intimate to me, are linked to patriarchal or capitalist facets within the home. Reflecting on your discussion about "fake intimate spaces" in studios, how does this widespread creation of content from personal spaces, often staged, impact the audience's intimacy? Does the media influence extend to this sense of intimacy, shaping perceptions of domesticity?

NICHOLAS Much of my work on domestic space stems from a Marxist feminist perspective. I refer to writers such as Silvia Federici, Mariarosa Dalla Costa, and I am trying to translate their political understanding of domestic labor, which is embedded in patriarchal culture, into the spatial practice of decorating. I first tried to work on that in parallel: the idea of home as a factory and the question of representation, of the discovery of self-expression. At first, I thought self-expression was a way of concealing this labor. But it is more complicated than that and it got me into the work of the late Foucault. The idea is how this subject both creates domestic space but is also created by it.
Home is always something that you see both "done," like a verb, and also something that is always being represented. And I think this is partially because of the weird theological consideration of the relationship between home and subject as a representation of it. The radical transformation in how we perceive spaces happened with the webcam on the phone, the single-point perspective. Influencers are an economic category, a representation of an increasing precarity that makes yourself and your image the only thing that you have to sell. And then, the home becomes a canvas to make their value visible. When we consider the home, we explore ways to present ourselves as valuable, in a logic that mirrors the financial market.

ILARIA There is this friction between the display and the construction of the self in the house in relation to specific domestic items. How is this process happening?

NICHOLAS We put pressure on the notion of the self as something that is an intact, stable thing that can fully be expressed. One can reverse it and say that

They asked me to design a house,

the self as domestic space is something that is produced through media and labor. It is about what we say the self is. Sometimes when I teach, the students are frustrated because they feel their work has to be an expression of themselves, but that's not true; *they* feel that they have to express themselves. So, we look into identity categories, and forces like solidarity or community alliances. Psychoanalysis is a helping structure, in saying that every act of declaring "I" is also an act of declaring "we." A political argument I have in my work is that if we understand that home is a site of labor, but also that decorating leads to mass consumption, then at the same time, we have to relearn how to inhabit the existence.
This is also true for the self. We figure out how to express ourselves with a language that is borrowed. We are not inventing our language all the time, we are constantly citing and quoting everyone from our parents, friends, what we read, and so on. It is an assemblage of citations and so is the home, I think. We need to politically put pressure on the mandate of having a self that is visible, legible, and acceptable by this matrix.

GEORGINA I am interested in your book *The Uses of Decorating.* The debate over whether decoration is associated with femininity is extensive within the field of interior design. It raises questions about distinguishing between design initiatives and mere decoration.

NICHOLAS The book actually begins with the phrase "mere decorating." So, where does this come from? In my book, I located it as a disparagement of the decorator, which would be the woman. I am not sure that's true. I think you can also say that it comes from a bigger preoccupation that hunts Western thinking between the essential and the appearance.
Recently, I have been interested in the writings of Anne Anlin Cheng. She is a literary theorist, but she wrote extensively about Josephine Baker, for whom Adolf Loos designed a house. She also had an affair with Le Corbusier. In her writing, she reverses the typical interpretation advanced by Colomina, which portrays Baker as a victim of white misogynists. She was a dancer. Anne says that modernists were jealous of her ability to render modernity through appearance, through the theatricality of a performance. For me, architecture is very rarely well-illuminated by architecture historians and theorists; it is better approached by sociologists, anthropologists, and literally theorists.

ILARIA How do you challenge this multidisciplinarity in your teaching?

NICHOLAS In my lectures, I often highlight a paradox in Western architectural thought. Architects frequently seek external validation for their work, responding to economic and power structures. At the same time, they often adopt elements of Western philosophy in an attempt to legitimize their formal practices. Take Laugier and his Primitive Hut, for example; his argument is deeply influenced by Rousseau and Hobbes, reflecting their notions of

civilization. On the other hand, both Hobbes and Rousseau use the idea of buildings to support their theories on how society should function. This creates a fragile semantic connection, where architecture and philosophical concepts are intertwined in ways that can feel disconnected or inconsistent.
Another important point for me to teach is that modernism is not a monolithic concept. While figures like Adolf Loos present aesthetically pleasing buildings, their ideologies pose several challenges. Conversely, the same period includes Margarete Schütte-Lihotzky and radical thinkers striving for communal living solutions. In teaching Architecture History, I delve into ancient and medieval thinking, revealing that normative beliefs perceived as modernist are often older and rooted in Catholic theological construction. Rather than viewing modernism as a form of progressive development, we should examine the role of the figure of the savage throughout modernist thinking. When I teach, the question is to understand how the arguments are structured and used to defend why we practice the way we do. If we can deconstruct these arguments, examine their foundations, and realize that these foundations are self-reliant, then we can start questioning the normative beliefs we have about our practice, such as the idea that an architect should design how people live rather than designing around how people live.

ILARIA I believe it's essential to foster a culture of sharing methodologies, aligning with the approach you promote through your teaching. I am worried that interdisciplinary collaboration may become more of a trend rather than a sustained practice with meaningful impact.

NICHOLAS I often wonder why we limit discussions on building or interior projects to architects and clients. Why not let decolonizing thinkers explain decolonization? One of the best functions of this discipline is its ability to bridge disciplines. Architecture should engender conversations and involve different stakeholders from various disciplines, as well as those who have to live with the structures we create. To paraphrase Adolfo Natalini, architecture should disappear, and I think that would be the best goal; to disappear and become a bridge between different discourses.

They asked me to design a house,

Figure 1
A screenshot of an empty video feed on the adult webcam site Chaturbate.

Figure 2
A room from the virtual tour of Studio20. Source: Nicholas Korody. Copyright: not definitively determined.

Nicholas asked them to design a home

NICHOLAS KORODY is a writer, editor, designer, and researcher. With Victoria Camblin he runs the consulting agency Magazine Capital, and he is the co-founder of the design research studio Adjustments Agency with Joanna Joseph. He is currently the lecturer in architectural history and theory at Amsterdamse Hogeschool voor de Kunsten as well as an instructor in the Social Design department of the Design Academy Eindhoven. He is the author of a collection of essays titled *The Uses of Decorating,* which was translated into Spanish and published in Madrid in 2020. He formerly served as Managing Editor of the Milan-based design magazine *Capsuleand* was the founding Editor-in-Chief of the architecture magazine *Ed* published by Archinect. His writing has been featured in publications such as *032c, Pin-Up, Harvard Design Magazine, Metropolis, GQ Middle East,* and *e-flux Architecture*, while his visual work has been exhibited at institutions internationally, including M+ Museum in Hong Kong, Swiss Institute in New York, Triennale di Milano, Musée d'art moderne de la Ville de Paris, the Moderna Museet in Stockholm, and the V-A-C Zattere in Venice.

They asked me to design a house,

How to Teach Someone to Design a Home (?)

Georgina Pantazopoulou

UNDER THE CARPET

75
Jean Baudrillard, *The System of Objects* (London: Verso Books, 2020), 14.

"What gives the houses of our childhood such depth and resonance in memory is clearly this complex structure of interiority, and the objects within it serve for us as boundary markers of the symbolic configuration known as home."
Baudrillard, *The System of Objects*[75]

From a very young age, I've been mesmerized by the idea of houses – not just as physical structures, but as homes and spatial spheres that hold stories and reflect the identities of their inhabitants. Even before I fully understood what architecture was (probably around the age of seven), I dreamed of designing homes that felt alive with personal meaning – spaces that were not only functional but deeply connected to the lives of those who lived in them. I imagined homes not as static or neutral places, but as dynamic environments filled with emotional resonance, where walls, furniture, and objects engaged in an open, even playful, dialogue with their users. This fascination wasn't just about creating shelters, but about designing spaces that felt familiar and nurtured a sense of belonging and identity. For many architecture students, this might sound like a typical idealization of the field, but for me, it has remained a core belief – one that continues to inform and inspire my work.

When I first began studying architecture, I quickly realized that much of the focus was on technical skills and building functionality. Many projects prioritized making a building "work" in the most efficient and practical way, often at the expense of exploring its deeper emotional or social impact. My early projects were shaped by these functional requirements, but they rarely considered who would be using the space, how they would interact with it, or why it truly mattered. I started to feel that the deeper connections I had envisioned between design and personal experience were being overlooked. This gap in my education became increasingly apparent, yet at the time, I wasn't fully equipped to address it. The dream of creating spaces that resonated with people's lived experiences –

spaces that fostered a true sense of home and belonging – remained, but it felt distant.

As I progressed in my studies, I began to question the narrow focus of architecture – particularly interior architecture – and its tendency to prioritize function over lived experience. What does it truly mean to design a home, a space where people not only live but genuinely feel at home? Could architecture reflect the complexities of people's identities – their cultural, social, and emotional dimensions– rather than just their functional needs? These questions gradually became central to my research, leading me to explore domesticity as a critical lens for rethinking equality and inclusivity, especially within interior design education. Over time, I came to understand that the concept of "domesticity" is far more intricate than it initially appears, carrying deep social and cultural implications that shape the way we experience space.

Figure 1
Outside the yard with you and someone else. Illustration, Georgina Pantazopoulou, 2023. Copyright: Georgina Pantazopoulou.

They asked me to design a house,

In *Queer Phenomenology*, Sara Ahmed suggests that orientation is not just about finding one's way in space but about how we come to "feel at home" in that space.[76] The feeling of being at home is deeply connected to the emotional and psychological dimensions of space – it is about belonging, not just to a place but also to the people and communities we share it with. Ahmed's work highlights the dynamic relationship between space and identity, showing how our environments shape who we are and how we, in turn, shape them to reflect our sense of self. This is where architecture and interior design intersect with broader questions of identity, inclusion, and power.

76 Sara Ahmed, *Queer Phenomenology: Orientations, Objects, Others* (Durham, NC: Duke University Press, 2006).

As scholars like Chiara Briganti and Kathy Mezei suggest, the concept of domestic space extends far beyond the physical structure of a house, home, or garden. It encompasses the social, psychological, spiritual, and political dimensions that shape our experience of these spaces. A home is not just where we live – it is where we construct our sense of self, define our relationships with others, and navigate the broader social, cultural, and political forces that influence our lives. This makes domestic space a deeply charged site, not only in terms of design but also in its role in reinforcing or challenging social norms and power dynamics.

The ideas of home and domesticity have long been shaped by gendered expectations, influencing both cultural norms and architectural design. Architectural historian Hilde Heynen examines how domesticity emerged as a set of gendered constructs that reinforced the separation between work and home.[77] Traditionally, domestic space was feminized, closely tied to women's roles as caregivers, while public and workspaces were masculinized. These divisions were not merely cultural – they were physically embedded in the design of homes. Kitchens and nurseries, for instance, were often relegated to the "private" areas of the house, reinforcing the perception of women's work as invisible and separate from public life. Such spatial arrangements reflected and reinforced deep-seated beliefs about gender roles – about what was considered "natural" for men and women and how those roles were inscribed in architectural design.[78]

77 Hilde Heynen and Gülsüm Baydar, eds., *Negotiating Domesticity: Spatial Productions of Gender in Modern Architecture* (London: Routledge, 2005).

78 Beatriz Colomina and Jennifer Bloomer, *Sexuality & Space* (New York: Princeton Architectural Press, 1992).

However, feminist theorists like Iris Marion Young, in her essay *House and Home: Feminist Variations on a Theme*, argue that domesticity is a dynamic, evolving concept – one that shapes both personal and collective identity in a fluid, material way. Young emphasizes that homemaking is not just physical labor but also an act of creativity, identity formation, and social connection. Domesticity serves as a site of personal agency, where gender roles, family structures, and power dynamics are continuously negotiated. Yet, despite its profound influence on identity and community, domesticity remains largely overlooked or marginalized in architectural discourse.

I have encountered this marginalization firsthand in my academic and professional journey. Despite its centrality to everyday life, domesticity is often treated as a secondary concern in architectural education. The focus tends to be on large-scale projects, public buildings, or the technical aspects of design, rather than the intimate, personal spaces we call home. Yet, as scholars like Lilian Chee emphasize, home is far more than just a private dwelling – it is an intersection of space, power, and identity, a site where larger societal structures take shape.[79] When design education overlooks these complexities, it misses the opportunity to reimagine what home can be – not just as a physical space but as a force for inclusivity, empathy, and social justice, as well as creativity and imagination.

This gap in the curriculum has driven me to explore domestic design through an intersectional feminist lens. Feminist pedagogy in architecture has the potential to radically reshape how we teach and practice design by fostering more inclusive and empathetic approaches. It challenges traditional power dynamics – between teacher and student, client and architect, theory and practice – by advocating for a design process that is collaborative, participatory, and attuned to the needs of diverse communities. At its core, feminist design pedagogy recognizes that architecture is not just about buildings but about people, their identities, and their lived experiences. In doing so, it also confronts dominant design paradigms that have historically excluded or marginalized certain groups, particularly women, people of color, and other minority communities.

As Kimberlé Crenshaw's work on intersectionality suggests, no approach to design can be fully effective unless it accounts for the ways that gender, race, age, class, and ability intersect to shape people's experiences.[80] A truly inclusive design practice, then, must

79
Lilian Chee, "Domesticity, Gender, and Architecture", in *The Routledge Companion to Contemporary Architectural History, ed. Duanfang Lu* (New York: Routledge, 2023).

80
And this makes me believe that feminist theory has a crucial role to play in rethinking the design of domestic spaces.

They asked me to design a house,

engage with the complex realities of identity and experience, going beyond the "default" user pattern of the white, cisgender, able-bodied individual.[81] When we approach design from an intersectional feminist perspective, we open up new possibilities for reimagining spaces that are inclusive and supportive of everyone, regardless of their gender, race, age, class, or ability.

81
Kimberle Crenshaw, 'Mapping the Margins: Intersectionality, Identity Politics, and Violence against Women of Color', *Stanford Law Review* 43, no. 6 (1991): 1241–99.

The tools we use to design domestic spaces must evolve to reflect this shift. Architectural and interior design methods often rely heavily on technical drawings – floor plans, sections, and 3D models – which are valuable for visualizing spatial relationships but frequently overlook the lived experiences of users. These methods can sometimes feel impersonal or inaccessible, especially to those unfamiliar with architectural language. As Harriet Harriss and Naomi House argue in *Interiority Complex*, interior design requires more than just technical expertise – it demands emotional intelligence, the ability to read both people and buildings, and an understanding of how space shapes lives.[82] This kind of sensitivity to the lived experience of space is crucial if we are to design environments that truly feel like home, spaces that foster belonging and inclusivity.

82
Harriet Harriss and Naomi House, 'Interiority Complex', in *A Gendered Profession* (RIBA Publishing, 2019).

Figure 2
Re-constructing domesticity in Kythira. Illustration-collage, Georgina Pantazopoulou, 2023. Copyright: Georgina Pantazopoulou.

Georgina asked them to design a home

But how do we teach someone to design a home? Interior architecture education – particularly interior design studios – offers a vital space to rethink and reshape how design is taught and practiced. These studios provide an opportunity to foster a more inclusive, socially aware, and culturally sensitive approach to design education. As the heart of interior architecture, the design studio is not just a place for creative exploration; it is where students engage with peers, absorb knowledge, and critically reflect on the design process itself. The design studio is the place where "creative exploration is conducted, interaction is encouraged, and a context is provided for the acquisition of knowledge, its assimilation through the design process, and reflection upon the insights gained."[83] The aim is to shift the focus from the designer and architect's intentions to the real-life needs and experiences of users, ensuring that design responses are rooted in actual human experiences, rather than theoretical ideals. This move away from universal design principles is crucial, as the idea of universalism tends to overlook and marginalize what is seen as different or *other*.[84] By exploring domesticity from a radical perspective, we can begin to see how an intersectional feminist approach might reveal the home as a dynamic, ever-changing space. As bell hooks[85] suggests, the home is not just a static place but a site for discovering new ways of living and engaging with each other; ways that embrace diversity, change, and multiple perspectives.

83 Laura Sanderson and Sally Stone, eds., *Emerging Practices in Architectural Pedagogy: Accommodating an Uncertain Future* (New York: Routledge, 2021), 5.

84 Alison Place, *Feminist Designer: On the Personal and the Political in Design* (Cambridge, MA: MIT Press, 2023).

85 bell hooks, 'Choosing the Margin as a Space of Radical Openness', *Framework: The Journal of Cinema and Media*, no. 36 (1989): 15–23.

Figure 3
Re-designing my grandmother's house. Part of my graduation project "Her Practice: Biases, Glitches and Oppressive Values or a Happy Domesticity" for Royal Academy of Art The Hague, 2022. Photo Credits and Copyright: Georgina Pantazopoulou.

They asked me to design a house,

To design a home, one must first understand what it truly means to feel at home. It is about cultivating intimacy and familiarity – imagining that deep sense of comfort and warmth that comes from being in a space where you feel loved, safe, and protected. A home is more than just a shelter; it is a space of resistance, a place where we can be ourselves and reclaim our identities. Interior architects must approach the design of these intimate spaces with great sensitivity, treating walls and materials with care, as if every gesture is a delicate one. It is about envisioning the daily rhythms – the shared meals, the light filtering through the windows, the quiet moments that shape our lives. Designing a home is an act of creating new worlds, and with that comes a responsibility: to be deeply respectful of the people who will inhabit these spaces, the people who will turn walls, windows, and doors into a home.

GEORGINA PANTAZOPOULOU (she/her) is a Greek multidisciplinary artist, architect, and researcher, currently based between Antwerp and Athens. As a PhD candidate at the University of Antwerp in the Faculty of Design Sciences, she is also a member of the Henry van de Velde Research Group. Her work critically examines the contemporary role of domesticity, challenging the legacy of modernism through an intersectional feminist lens. Georgina co-founded the research and design duo Common Ground Practice, which focuses on creating safe spaces for marginalized communities and fostering new, dominant memories within spatial practices. She holds a Master's in Interior Architecture from the Royal Academy of Art in The Hague and a Master's in Architecture from the University of Patras. Her practice spans text, drawings, illustrations, and performances.

They asked me to design a house,

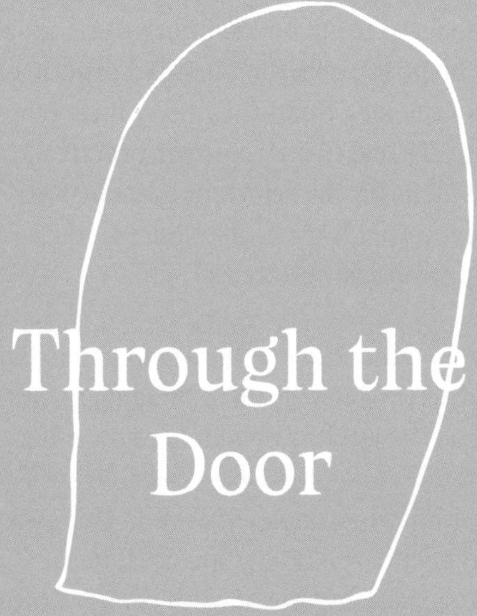

Through the Door

Sophia Pekowsky
Vida Rucli
Ramón Jiménez Cárdenas
Setareh Noorani
Susanna Tomassini
Rising Lai
Ilaria Palmieri

INTRODUCTION

What does it mean to dwell together in conditions shaped by displacement, precarity, or inherited structures of exclusion? How might practices of hospitality, kinship, and homemaking be reconfigured when the home itself is contested? The contributions gathered in this chapter invite us to think beyond normative ideals of the home, the family, and the host, proposing instead practices that embrace plurality and complexity. Spanning disciplines from architecture to video art, from critical theory to craft practice, the voices in this chapter share a focus on the relational dimensions of domestic life: how space is negotiated, care is distributed, roles are redefined, and routines are continuously adapted.

From the village of Topolò, Vida Rucli explores collective living as a feminist and ecological practice, inviting us to imagine hospitality as an act that re-centers care as the guiding principle of dwelling.

The attention to hospitality continues in Sophia Pekowsky's reflection on its emotional and gendered labor. She critiques traditional power dynamics in practicing hospitality that are often racialized, gendered, and classed. At the same time, she explores the potential for hospitality to become something more reciprocal and transformative, a site of connection and mutual vulnerability.

Susanna Tomassini explores how precarious housing conditions and the breakdown of traditional pathways to adulthood foster 'neotribal' kinships, where communal bonds are built through mutual care and shared responsibility. Her work challenges normative models of independence and adulthood, asking us to rethink what solidarity looks like in conditions of precarity and fragmentation.

Ramón Jiménez Cárdenas confronts the hegemonic structures of the nuclear family, particularly in its intersection with settler colonialism. He argues that the nuclear family, with its emphasis on

They asked me to design a house,

biological ties and heteronormative values, perpetuates neoliberal ideologies while marginalizing non-traditional kinship structures. His contribution calls for kinship beyond normative frameworks, challenging the structures that render hospitality – conditional and exclusionary.

Rising Lai challenges the cultural and symbolic dominance of the Red Sleeping Bed, a traditional Taiwanese marriage bed, demonstrating how even the most symbolically rigid domestic artifacts can be opened up to alternative desires and affiliations. Through collaborative engagements with artisans, Lai reimagines the bed – historically a symbol of heteronormative and patriarchal ideals – as a site for queerness, desire, and inclusion.

These critiques are further deepened in our conversation with Setareh Noorani, who shows how decolonial, feminist, and queer approaches to architecture challenge traditional roles of the architect and transform understandings of space. Drawing from her work at the Nieuwe Instituut, Setareh advances more inclusive, participatory, and care-centered narratives that foster spatial justice.

Ilaria Palmieri reflects on participatory design within contexts of forced migration. She critiques top-down, emergency-driven design models and calls instead for methods that recognize the agency and knowledge of displaced communities. Her work promotes the unlearning of inherited design paradigms and the development of more situated, context-responsive approaches.

What kinds of solidarity and cohabitation become possible when we loosen our attachment to permanence, ownership, and normative family structures? What might it mean to build homes not around possession or stability, but around relation, reciprocity, and shared transformation? This chapter gestures toward forms of dwelling that are responsive, adaptive, and continuously in-the-making, calling for more hospitable ways of inhabiting the world, especially in times of social and ecological fragility.

Through the door,

where

solidarity grows.

They asked me to design a house,

THROUGH THE DOOR

The Breathing House: Practices of Collective Dwelling on a Margin

Vida Rucli

"Zones of unpredictability at the edges of discursive stability, where contradictory discourses overlap, or where discrepant kinds of meaning-making converge; these are what I call margins."
Anna Tsing, 'From the Margins'[86]

"This is an invitation to a practice of radical hospitality – an opening up to all that is possible in the thickness of the Now in rejecting practices of a-void-ance, taking responsibility for injustices, activating and aligning with forces of justice, and welcoming the other in an undoing of the colonizing notion of self-hood rather than as a marker of not us, not me."
Karen Barad, 'After the End of the World'[87]

86
Anna Lowenhaupt Tsing, "From the Margins", *Cultural Anthropology* 9, no. 3 (1994): 279–97.

87
Karen Barad, "After the End of the World: Matters of Hospitality", In *Rehearsing Hospitalities: Companion 3*, edited by Yvonne Billimore and Jussi Koitela (Berlin: Archive Books, 2021).

Vida asked them to design a home

Dwelling on a margin

Topolò/Topolove[88] is a hamlet in the mountains, surrounded by a sea of trees, accessible only by a single road that ends at the village. Situated in northeastern Italy, just 300 meters from the Slovenian border, this village experienced a dramatic decline in population throughout the 20th century due to historical, geopolitical, and economic factors. At the start of the last century, it was home to 400 residents. Today, only 25 people live there year-round, occupying the same houses that once sheltered a thriving community. The village hosted for almost thirty years – from 1994 to 2022 – the art project and later art festival *Stazione di Topolò/Postaja Topolove*, which brought to the village hundreds of international and local artists, exploring questions of locality, identity, history, and contemporaneity. Alongside this festival, a group of children grew up there, and in 2017, they formed the Robida collective. Five members of the collective, including architects, teachers, and cultural producers – all around 30 years old – reside in Topolò. They engage in practices of situated cultural and editorial production, critically examining the role of rural areas in contemporary cultural discourse. Over the past decade, they have hosted friends, organized seminars and summer schools, published a magazine, and explored models for future ruralisms. The text that follows is written by me, Vida, one of the members and co-founders of the collective. Here – in the text and in the place where I am writing from – I explore, together with others, questions emerging from and revolving around our dwelling and cultural practice: questions on feminist hospitality, spatial responsibility, interspecies spaces, and collective maintenance.

88 Topolò, named in Slovene language Topolove, is a village of the municipality of Grimacco (Udine). It belongs to the borderland area of Valli del Natisone/Nediške doline, inhabited by the Slovene minority, hence its double name.

Figure 1
Academy of Margins, 2022. Photo Credits: Elena Rucli. Copyright: Robida.

They asked me to design a house,

The metropolis of birds

"In this sense, it is important to think about the collective as an activity. To approach the notion of collectives not as a pre-existing social structure but as actively becoming in context. So that becoming a collective is an acting toward it, a coming together and dissolving and recomposing."

Jeanne van Heeswijk, 'Preparing for the Not-Yet'[89]

When Bianca, a designer and researcher of community economies and commons in the alpine territories, stepped out of her car in Topolò the first time, she was flooded by the dense, multilayered sound of an interspecific choir of birds,[90] singing at the sunset on an early spring day. The place where she parked the car has the remarkable quality of magnifying sounds (years ago it was even used as an auditorium for a symphonic orchestra) and the experience there truly felt like being immersed in a symphony of thousands of singing birds. Topolò is often seen as a periphery – a village perched on the edge of a man-made border, at the end of a solitary road, home to just twenty-five residents. A place that has seen only departures. A topographic, geographic, and cultural margin. "But the periphery of what?" asked Bianca during a talk, part of our "Academy of Margins" program,[91] "This is the metropolis of wildlife!", she continued. The dense, young, and humble forest embraces the village and it is lively inhabited by all species of animals, which we share some liminal spaces with. These are spaces where the village merges into the forest, becoming a forest itself in the ruins of old houses, abandoned fields once used for agriculture, paved paths, and old dry-stone walls. Ancestral traces of human inhabitation make space for lively communities or vegetal and animal beings.

I walk through the forest that surrounds Topolò. I follow the old paths along the tall stone walls that have been covered with moss and ivy over time. Near the river, I once noticed narrow, slightly meandering paths emerging near some ruins. Initially, I assumed they were remnants of the old trails villagers once used to reach their fields and meadows. However, it soon became evident that these paths were not created by the village's human residents but by roe deer. The narrow path I walked by when I went to the river was the one that the deer were crossing every day to reach the water. I recognized it; it was narrower than human paths and descended diagonally along

89 [H]eeswijk, Jeanne van. [']Preparing for the Not-[Y]et". In *Slow Reader: [A] Resource for Design [T]hinking and Practice*, [e]dited by Ana Paula Pais [a]nd Carolyn F. Strauss [(]Amsterdam: Valiz, 2016).

90 [I] can only suppose it [w]as an interspecific [c]hoir of birds. More on [t]his phenomenon can [b]e found in Malavasi, [R]achele, and Almo [F]arina. "Neighbours Talk: [I]nterspecific Choruses [a]mong Songbirds". *[B]ioacoustics* 22, no. 1 (12 [A]ugust 2012): 33–48; [D]espret, Vinciane. *Living [a]s a Bird (*Cambridge: [P]olity, 2021*)*.

91 [T]he *Academy of Margins* [i]s one of Robida's [p]rojects. It is a learning [p]rogram, initiated in 2022 and structured [a]round a summer school, [s]eminars, reading groups [a]nd workshops, which [r]e-thinks Topolò as a [l]earning site, rather than [o]nly as a background for [e]vents.

the ridge, parallel to the stream. There were no plants growing on it, which meant that deer probably used it every day.
History is described by Anna Tsing as a "record of many world-making trajectories."[92] And how beautiful it is to notice that our own trajectories intersect with the desired lines of deer, birds, ants, and ivy. The *dear old forgotten paths* are now the *deer's paths.*

In the village, we negotiate the roles of hosts and guests with thorny brambles, ants, and salamanders. We share a reciprocal hospitality with the creepers, hornets, and beech martens, sometimes letting them take more space than we wish and gently invading some of theirs in exchange. In winter, we allow brambles, weeds, and lianas to thrive in the garden. Then, in early spring, when it is time to start planting vegetables for the summer, we softly renegotiate their position and ours, trimming them and year after year attempting to redraw the borders between the garden and the wilderness. This edge between the village and the forest, between the vegetable garden and the brambles' intricate mass, is unclear, nonlinear, always moving: expanding and withdrawing. Lingering at this threshold, where hosts and guests seamlessly exchange roles, invites us to reimagine the possibilities of interspecies spaces – what they could look like, how they could function, and how they might be nurtured and preserved.

92 Anna Lowenhaupt Tsing, *The Mushroom at the End of the World: On the Possibility of Life in Capitalist Ruins* (Princeton University Press, 2015).

Figure 2 Care of Margin symposium, 2021. Photo Credits and Copyright: Robida.

They asked me to design a house,

The breathing house

"How does a gathering become a "happening," that is, greater than a sum of its parts? One answer is contamination. We are contaminated by our encounters; they change who we are as we make way for others. As contamination changes world-making projects, mutual worlds – and new directions – may emerge."

Anna Tsing, *The Mushroom at the End of the World* [93]

93 Tsing, Mushroom at the End of the World, 27.

In the summer, our houses are corridors, squares, public bathrooms, common kitchens. The dining room is the green lot with a big table in front of one of our houses, the only outdoor shadowy space, which in the evenings becomes a cinema. The living room is the small pebbled streets, the stone stairs in front of an abandoned house, the low walls, the garden. The shower is the stream in the valley below the village. In the winter, the whole house becomes the only heated room. Life is still, and in this stillness, we plan and desire the fullness, commonality, publicness of summers. What we use and understand as a house is cyclically expanding and retracting with the rhythm of the temperature. A wide, branched-out, decentralized and interconnected house in summer. An intimate curled-up space in winter. As the seasons shift, our house breathes with the changing temperatures. Alongside this fluctuation in the perceived volume of our home, our acts of care also follow the rhythm of these seasonal movements. In winter, it's about cleaning the stove, reorganizing indoor spaces, and fixing small things. In summer, it involves digging the garden, sweeping the streets, weeding the paths, and tending to the forest. Together, we practice the care of the village, considering its public spaces, abandoned ruins, ruderal landscapes, and the spaces in between as an extension of our home.

In the processes of dwelling collectively in the village, considering it our house, practicing the commoning of tools and infrastructure, and sharing resources, knowledge, and spaces, we are frequently joined by temporary inhabitants, friends, and passers-by who actively become part of these everyday practices. The rhythms of people arriving in Topolò and those of us living here year-round merge into polyrhythmic patterns that, over time, become synchronized. Every year, when spring causes the rooms to expand and occupy the outdoor space and landscape, the breathing house opens its doors to temporary inhabitants who live with the permanent community for a short period, cyclical inhabitants who return year after year, and seasonal inhabitants who use their houses only during specific seasons. Those permanently living in the village are joined by those visiting, who share and take part in the caretaking activities, the practices of everyday life, and the rhythms of the space. Through these interactions, the definition of hospitality and the relationship between hosts and guests are softened, shaped by this way of engaging with space.

Hospitality is traditionally understood as a hierarchical and unidirectional concept. However, following its etymology, it was originally conceived as a reciprocal movement of visiting and being visited. The Latin word *hospes, -ĭtis*, from which *hospitality* is derived, originally meant both *host* and *guest.* This dual meaning arose because hosting someone traditionally implied the expectation of being hosted in return. The reciprocal nature of hospitality thus gave rise to the word's double meaning, a polysemy that also persists in the Italian word *ospite.*[94] Despite the original reciprocity implied in the term, traditionally, the host *actively* gives, while the guest *passively* receives. The host *hosts*, while the guest can only *be hosted.* While opening our houses and sharing them with friends, we try to reverse this movement of giving and receiving: Friends are not guests, they become co-inhabitants sharing small everyday responsibilities with us. The fragmented, decentralized, branched-out house expands even more when temporary inhabitants join us in the village, and daily tasks are shared with them, while maintenance actions are many times initiated by them.

94
More about the etymology of the terms host and guest can be found here: Angela Frati and Stefania Iannizzotto, 'Chi è effettivamente l'ospite', *Accademia Della Crusca* (blog), luglio 2012, https://accademiadellacrusca.it/it/consulenza/chi-%C3%A8-effettivamente-lospite/719.

What does hospitality mean in a different way of intending, administering, and taking care of private property? Could the articulation of *feminist* hospitality help transcend the oppressive gender legacy of traditional hospitality, where men were the property owners and women performed acts of hospitality? A softer and more fluid way of understanding the categories of private, public, and common stimulates practices of *mutual* and *reciprocal* hospitality. When the borders between private and public spaces blur, between the intimate and the open, the common and the personal, when a house becomes a corridor to walk through to reach a commonly used balcony, when everyday tools are shared and used collectively, when it is not clear who owns certain things or who is taking care of certain places, then sharing responsibilities, distributing tasks, and

They asked me to design a house,

disseminating caregiving roles become a collective effort.

By reinventing the structure of the house, reclaiming it "as the center of collective life"[95] rather than as a private, intimate space, and fostering a sense of shared ownership through the extension and distribution of care and maintenance practices with humans and non-humans, we rooted ourselves in a breathing house within a metropolis of birds.

95 Silvia Federici, *Re-Enchanting the World: Feminism and the Politics of the Commons* (Oakland, CA: PM Press, 2018).

Figure 3
Bee workshop, 2022. Photo Credits: Teo Giovanni Poggi. Copyright: Robida.

Vida asked them to design a home

Figure 4–5
Academy of Margins 2022, 2023. Photo Credits: Elena Rucli. Copyright: Robida.

Figure 6
Bee workshop, 2022. Photo Credits: Teo Giovanni Poggi. Copyright: Robida.

They asked me to design a house,

Vida asked them to design a home

VIDA RUCLI is an architect and cultural worker based in the village of Topolò/Topolove, situated on the borderland between Italy and Slovenia. She is editor of Robida Magazine (2014-) and co-curator for Robida's public programmes and projects (2017-). She lectured in different universities, collaborated with the festival *Climate Care* (Floating University, Berlin, 2023) and is a member of the international research group *Ecologies of Care* and of *Floating ~~University~~*, Berlin.

They asked me to design a house,

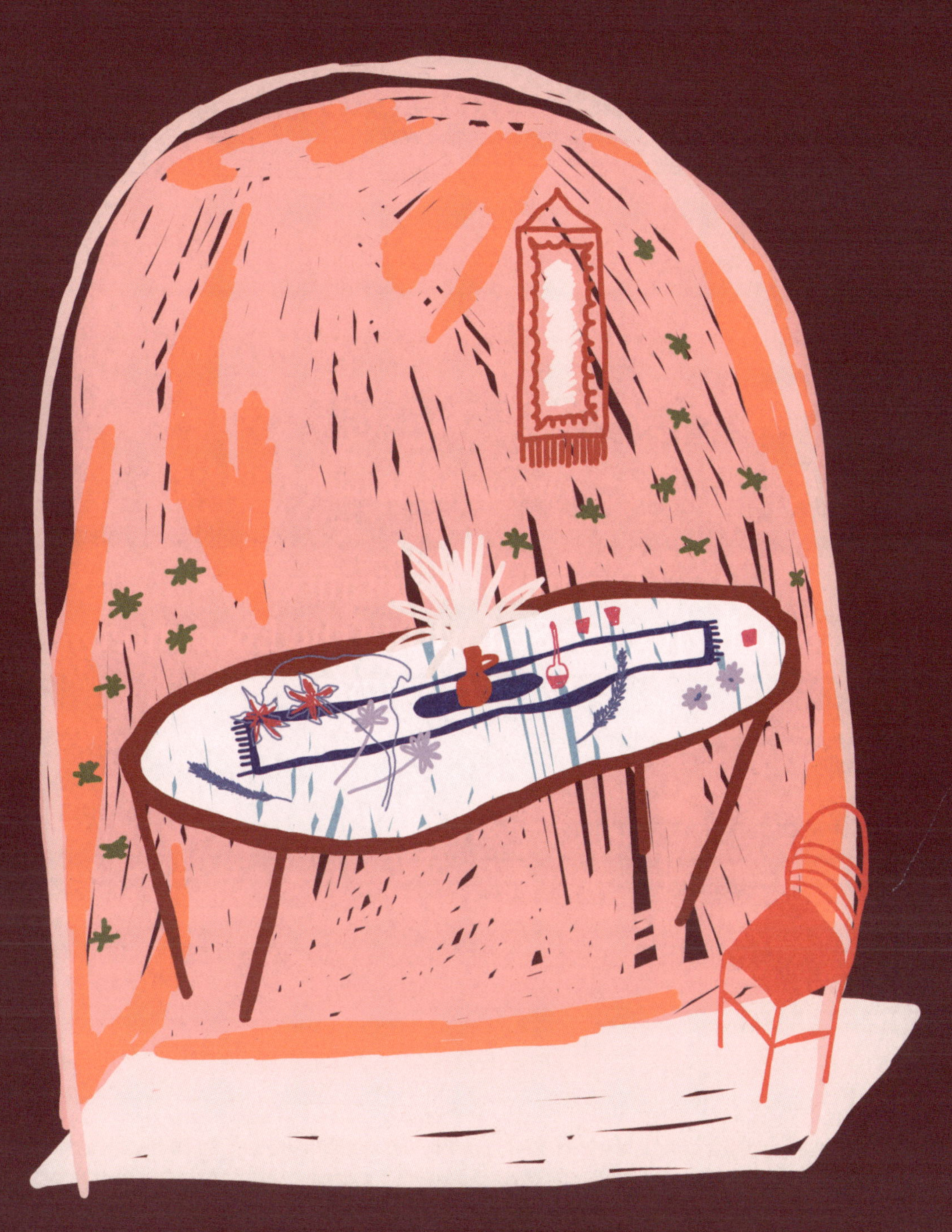

THROUGH THE DOOR

Feminist Hospitality: Stabilizing the Self within the Encounter

Sophia Pekowsky

Put the tea on to boil and measure out the correct amount of coffee; no more, no less. Ascertain how many cups and mugs you will need. Slice segments of lemon and place them in the water pitcher, along with fresh sprigs of mint. Arrange a tray of cookies to create a cascading effect. Splay out some clementines in between. To be a good hostess is to have a mind split into two overlapping glass windows, simultaneously listening and anticipating, relaxed and alert, smiling in response to an anecdote, and ready at any moment to jump into the kitchen to refill the water, with eyes flickering between eyes and hands, and between hands and mouths.

I came to be a part of this anthology through a lino printmaking workshop that I host at De Voorkamer, a community center in Utrecht that "works with creative processes and cultural practices to develop an inclusive space, with the goal of bridging the gaps between different groups in society."[96] The free workshops generally host an eclectic mixture of students, asylum seekers, pensioners, young professionals, the unemployed, and countless other people with overlapping identities that are hard to quantify and vary depending on the day, united on some level by a desire for connection through the arts. Every session is different and presents unique challenges in hospitality, such as: Is it possible to create a space where everyone feels welcome? Do we want a space where literally everyone feels welcome?

96 https://devoorkamer.org/.

I find that throughout our conversations, I am embodying hospitality as we discuss it, hospitality oozes from my toenails and my pores. It usually fills me up with a soft warmth inside, this "dance" of hospitality. But other times, the warmth becomes too hot and I feel itchy and resentful. I am afraid to admit that my sense of self has become intertwined with being a good hostess. I'm not sure when or how it started, I only know it wasn't always this way and that I don't want to be like this anymore. When I was a child, guests were an exciting addition to the familiar dynamics of my household. A visitor brought with them stories, presents, and new rhythms, but I noticed the sigh of relief from my parents when they left which surprised me because I didn't know they were tired to begin with. That's when I realized that to be "a good host/ess" is to appear effortless and it is this very process of appearing effortless that can make hosting so utterly draining.

At De Voorkamer, the discussions bend, turn, and move freely between different layers of hospitality – personal, professional, and political, which are all sticky threads impossible to separate. We discuss the power dynamics of hosting nations in the context of asylum seekers, the difficulty of being both a host and a guest, the expectation as a guest to show gratitude and the expectation of a host to burn themselves out for the guest, the creation of a customer service persona when working in hospitality, and different hosting expectations in different cultures. Before these discussions, I never thought about how many different spheres the concept of hospitality penetrates.

At the center of the discussion lies a central dilemma: The boundary between the self and the other, and the power dynamics that hospitality can either reinforce or challenge. The very premise of the host and the guest implies an explicit boundary between the self and the other. If that boundary is removed, who is the host, and who is the guest? One participant in the workshops created a print that haunted me throughout these sessions, in which the words "guest" and "host" were combined to create the word "ghost."

The Self and the Other

Much of feminist theory has focused on questioning the boundary between where the self ends and where the other begins. Feminist thinkers such as Rosi Braidotti[97] and Sarah Ahmed[98] have discussed at length how the philosophical construction of the humanist self in opposition to the other has had incredibly damaging consequences throughout history. "The 'man' of humanism claimed to be universal while simultaneously depicting a white, European, and able-bodied male subject. The exclusion of the 'other' from this ideal served as the basis for colonial crimes of genocide, creating the hypocrisy of modern Western culture: built on the enslavement and oppression of the 'other' while simultaneously promoting values of democracy, freedom, and equality."[99]

97 Rosi Braidotti, *The Posthuman* (Cambridge: Polity, 2013).

98 Sara Ahmed, *Strange Encounters: Embodied Others in Post-Coloniality* (London: Routledge, 2000).

99 Sophia Pekowsky, 'Postpartum as Portal: Reimagining Western Conceptions of the Human Through Linocut Printmaking Workshops on Postpartum and Motherhood by Sophia Pekowsky, 1961950' (Master Thesis, 2022), 27.

They asked me to design a house,

The Western self is thus constructed in opposition to a non-Western other, without which the Western self cannot exist. Within this construction of the other, lies everything that the West fears within itself. Theories of relationality then, provide an alternative understanding of the self, in which the self is not static but is rather constantly activated and changing through encounters. These theories encourage us to embrace the "monstrous other"[100] both inside ourselves and around us.

If feminist theory encourages questioning the line between the self and the other, a feminist hospitality is hard to imagine, as hospitality is often based on re-establishing and reinscribing the power dynamics between the self and the other. Just the word "hospitality" itself, brings to my imagination a bright veneer surface that is rotting on the inside. Hospitality work, based on displays of warmth and care, is globally underpaid and undervalued. Another invocation, "southern hospitality," the quality of residents of the southern U.S. states to be especially hospitable, also shows this hypocrisy. Southern literature scholar Anthony Szczesiul, explores how southern hospitality has its roots in the plantation economy of the South, discussing how "racism cannot be separated from the antebellum social practices of southern hospitality; indeed, it was the labor of the slave that provided the master the leisure to be so hospitable."[101] Indeed, hospitality is imbued with racialized and gendered connotations. It's easy to be a good host/ess when someone else is cooking your food.

Much of the theoretical examination of hospitality has been undertaken by philosopher Jacques Derrida, who differentiates between conditional hospitality, which reinscribes existing power dynamics and solidifies the self/other divide, and "unconditional" or "pure hospitality" that seeks to rupture this divide. Derrida describes a "pure hospitality" that welcomes all newcomers at any cost possible.

Pure hospitality [...] may be terrible because the newcomer may be a good person, or may be the devil; but if you exclude the possibility that the newcomer is coming to destroy your house – if you want to control this and exclude in advance this possibility – there is no hospitality. For unconditional hospitality to take place you have to accept the risk of the other coming and destroying the place, initiating a revolution, stealing everything, or killing everyone.[102]

100 Margrit Shildrick, *Embodying the Monster: Encounters with the Vulnerable Self* (London: SAGE Publications, 2002).

101 Anthony Szczesiul, *The Southern Hospitality Myth. Ethics, Politics, Race, and American Memory* (Athens: University of Georgia Press, 2017), 10.

102 Jacques Derrida, *Of Hospitality* (Stanford, CA Stanford University Press, 2000), 70-71.

But I can't fully embrace Derrida's approach. I wonder about the specifics of Derrida's home-life situation. Who was cleaning his house? Who was taking care of his children? It's much easier to devote yourself to the visitor without resentment on a philosophical plane than on a practical one.

Typically, the mechanics of hosting is women's work. Cooking, cleaning, making sure there is extra toilet paper, coffee, and tea, and that the guest's favorite snacks are stocked up in the pantry and the fridge. Women's work is invisibilized, in that it is made invisible. Like many women, I struggle with creating boundaries and space for myself, and hosting often exacerbates this. The lack of personal space can make me grumpy and guilt prevents me from enjoying myself. The discussions I had in my gender studies class about embracing relationality were very different from the conversations I had in therapy, in which I focused on how to set boundaries and settle into myself before fully devoting myself to others, as Derrida would encourage.

Feminist Hospitality and Gentleness

Informed by Derrida's unconditional hospitality, Maurice Hamington imagines a feminist hospitality that "explores the antinomy between disruption and connection: The guest and host disrupt each other's lives sufficiently to allow for meaningful exchanges that foster interpersonal connections of understanding."[103] While less extreme than Derrida's call to invite violence into our homes for the sake of unconditional hospitality, Hamington's feminist hospitality focuses on the philosophical aspects of hospitality rather than the practical elements. In *Thresholds and Challenges: Hospitality as a Challenge*, the authors discuss how "very often, initial generosity gradually morphs into forms of resentment, if not blatant animosity, between hosts and guests."[104] That way, hospitality easily turns into hostility, even with the best of intentions.

French philosopher Anne Dufformentalle puts forth a theory of gentleness when thinking about hospitality, a way of being that can inform feminist hospitality in a practical sense, both within interpersonal and political host/guest relationships. She describes gentleness as "an enigma." Taken up in a double movement of welcoming and giving, it appears on the threshold of passages signed

103 Maurice Hamington, 'Toward a Theory of Feminist Hospitality', *Feminist Formations* 22, no. 1 (2010): 24.

104 Maëlle Jeanniard du Dot and Marie Mianowski, 'Introduction | Thresholds and Refuges: Hospitality as a Challenge', *ILCEA. Revue de l'Institut Des Langues et Cultures d'Europe, Amérique, Afrique, Asie et Australie*, no. 50 (1 March 2023): 3.

They asked me to design a house,

off by birth and death. Because it has its degrees of intensity, because it is a symbolic force, and because it has a transformative ability over things and beings, it is a power."[105] For Dufformentalle, "The opposite of gentleness is not brutality or violence itself, it is the counterfeit of gentleness: What perverts it by imitating it. All forms of compromise, diluted suavity, sentimental mush."[106] This force of counterfeit hospitality is one of the primary catalysts for resentment.

105
Anne Dufourmantelle and Catherine Malabou, *Power of Gentleness: Meditations on the Risk of Living*, trans. Katherine Payne and Vincent Sall (New York: Fordham University Press, 2018), 1.

106
Ibid, 58

While resentment sometimes builds up when hosting in various aspects of my own life, I also find moments of intense joy in hosting, and it's always in the most gentle moments. And this also implies a gentleness with myself as well. Because by being gentle with ourselves, we are gentle to the people around us. If the division between the self and others is not so cemented, it also means treating ourselves as we would our guest. The challenge is to remove the shiny veneer from hospitality and let the encounter inform us. To be informed by gentleness, to not let resentment eat us away, to lean into the performance of hospitality, and in doing so, subvert it. As Dufformentalle urges: "Gentleness goes beyond a relation of care, it is a way-of-being-in-the-world and as such it should be like a beacon in the dark to try and make our world more hospitable."

SOPHIA PEKOWSKY (USA) is a creative program manager, workshop facilitator, and researcher passionate about using art as a tool for education, reflection, research, and activism. She works as a program manager and gender studies professor at the Council for International Educational Exchange and organizes creative interventions related to textiles with the Crafting Resistance Collective. Nothing makes her happier than creating activist community art initiatives with her friends.

They asked me to design a house,

THROUGH THE DOOR

The Southern Thruway

Susanna Tomassini

In fifteen months I will live somewhere, I don't know where, with someone. I don't know who.

"The Southern Thruway" is a video installation realized in 2023 which addresses the living situations of young urban creative workers in a neoliberal context. The shared house, central to the narrative, becomes a lens through which themes like the housing crisis, individualism, and self-actualization are explored. This project weaves together personal stories, insights, and data to capture the intricate interplay of these issues, while suggesting the possibility of a radical and unconventional love emerging within the most ordinary spaces.

While researching the theme of shared households, I was reminded of a short story by Julio Cortázar that I read long ago, which ultimately inspired the title of my video installation: *The Southern Thruway.* This story, the opening piece in *All Fires the Fire*, explores the experience of being caught in a liminal moment - depicted by the author as a traffic jam.
Cortázar vividly portrays an oppressively hot highway where the heat feels unbearable, and the end of the traffic jam is nowhere in sight. The drivers can't even glimpse their destination (Paris), but

only see an endless line of cars and the sun reflecting off their metal roofs. The characters are referred to by their car brands, with the protagonists named Dauphine and 404. In this stifling scenario, days pass by and the drivers are forced to adapt and organize for survival. They assign roles, gather resources, and distribute them among themselves. As the standstill stretches on, life unfolds: some fall in love, others fight, a few die, and some abandon their cars to disappear into the fields beyond the highway.

When they started the car to go to the city they were just looking forward.

But now they are stuck, and they look around, other faces are as confused as theirs.

When the drivers first started their cars to head toward the city, their focus was straight ahead, fixed on their destination. But now, stuck in the jam, they find themselves looking around - at the humanity surrounding them.

In a way, I feel like I've been in a traffic jam of my own for quite some time. The shared household, which I once viewed as a necessary but temporary arrangement, is becoming increasingly difficult to escape. Everyone around me seems to be heading in the same direction - toward some form of economic success or personal achievement - but the road never seems wide enough for all of us to reach our goals. In this uncomfortable and seemingly stagnant position, I've decided to start looking around, much like the characters in the story. What defines the shared household? Who lives within it? How did we all end up here?

They asked me to design a house,

I just bought a new design book I won't read.
It makes my room look cooler.

Many generations have long sought to escape and redefine the norms of their times. Today, for many of them, that escape involves rejecting the 9-to-5 grind and the suburban nuclear family, instead flocking to big cities in pursuit of a more individualistic way of living. However, it's hard to ignore that today's creative workers often resemble the working class more than artists living outside society's rules. The "middle-class dream" is becoming increasingly unattainable, leaving urban professionals clinging to symbols of a bourgeois lifestyle that, in reality, they can no longer fully afford. While there are undeniable differences between these groups, the veneer of creativity fades when reduced to essentials: some people struggle to meet their basic needs, and others do not.

Susanna asked them to design a home

Future is an uncofortable word.

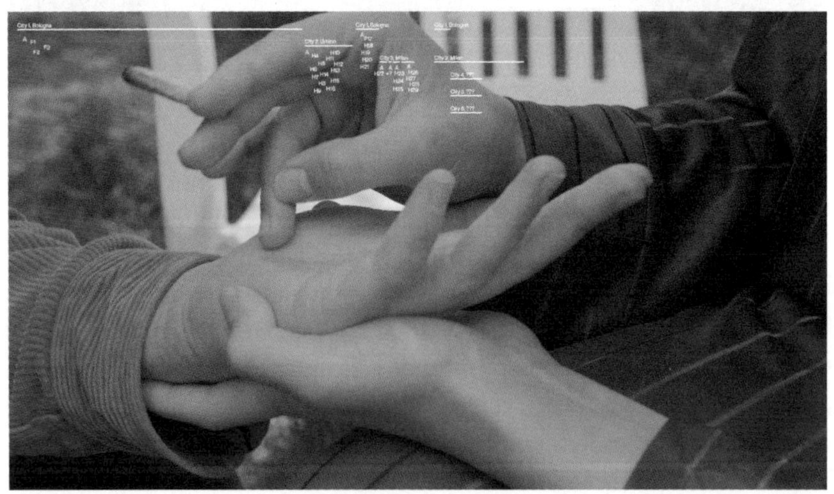

Everything sounds possible, everything sounds difficult.

They asked me to design a house,

Susanna asked them to design a home

They asked me to design a house,

In big cities, homes are no longer treated as basic human necessities but as commodities, exacerbating urban inequalities. Profit is prioritized over social needs, forcing lower-income individuals to pay more for substandard housing. This commodification of housing, coupled with the growing precarity of work conditions, leaves young workers uncertain about their futures. Though they may have more opportunities to change career paths, they lose the stability needed to make long-term plans. Not only must workers remain flexible in their skills, mindsets, and professional roles, but the boundaries between their social lives, leisure, personal interests, and professional identities are also increasingly blurred. This demand for flexibility in modern work and cultural environments results in frequent relocations, career shifts, and an endless pursuit of fulfillment and stability – one that often feels unattainable.

She feels like an adult,
she feels like an adolescent.
She says she has not idea
of what the fuck she will do in the future.

Susanna asked them to design a home

A certain intensity in amicable love is often seen as something related to youth. So moving, naive.

This lack of stability translates for many in a belated adulthood, at least as it was defined in the previous century. In this life frame, temporalities shift: some young adults are forced to continue living with their parents, while others spend years living alone or with roommates, frequently moving and exploring various career and educational opportunities. This extended liminal state raises an unsettling question: What does it mean to become an adult when the pathways we once associated with adulthood are no longer valid or accessible?

They asked me to design a house,

Stability gives me peace.

Being together makes me laugh.

Susanna asked them to design a home

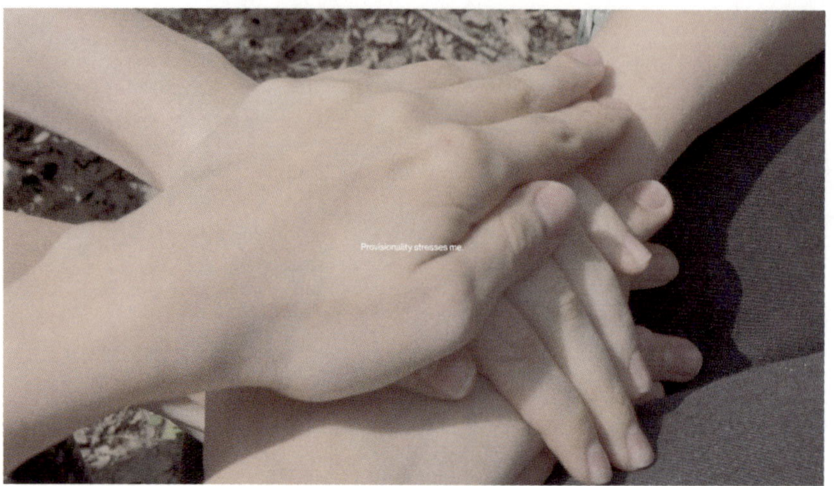

Provisionality stresses me.

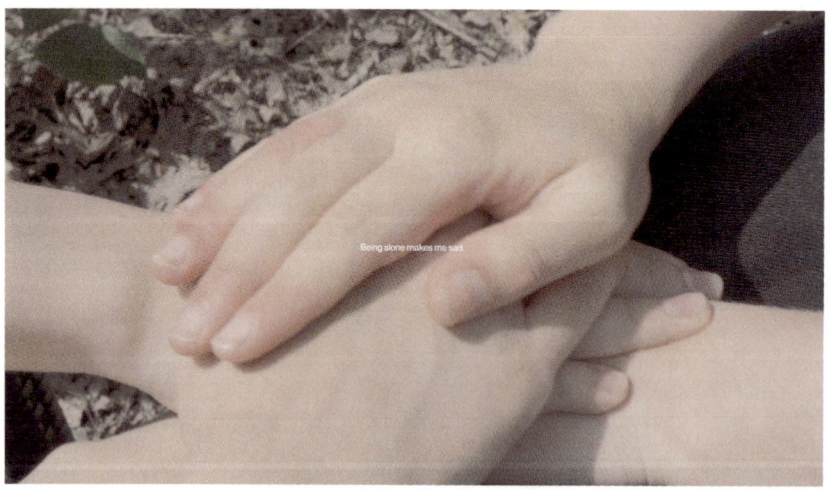

Being alone makes me sad.

They asked me to design a house,

Stability scares me.

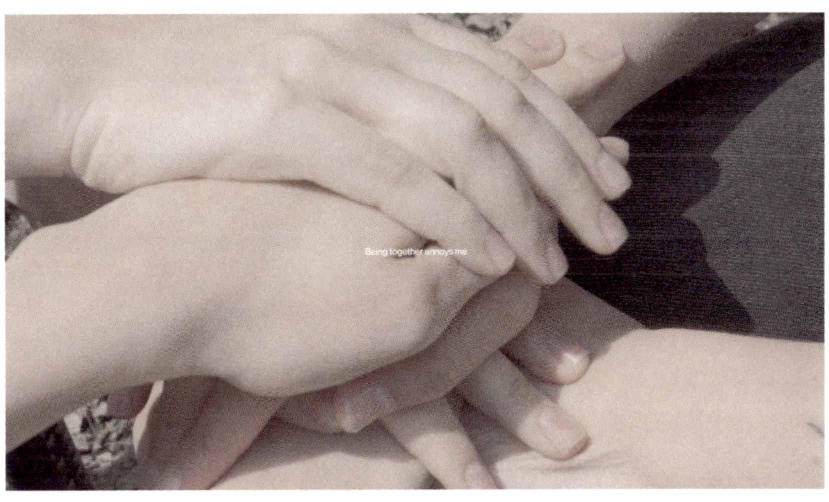

Being together annoys me.

Susanna asked them to design a home

Provisionality gives me novelty.

Being alone makes me breathe.

They asked me to design a house,

Work precarity and the housing crisis have made shared housing, though often undesirable, increasingly common for people in their twenties and thirties. Households have historically evolved alongside ideological and economic shifts: the nuclear family, for instance, emerged as a product of industrialization and urbanization, while communal living has, for centuries, served as a means of building communities, sharing reproductive labor, and addressing economic challenges. While modern shared households are often seen as symptoms of precarity and the housing crisis, could they also contain the seed of a new way of living? This question invites us to consider what these arrangements might signal about alternative paths forward.

The shared households in which I, and many others, find ourselves are clear indicators of specific economic and ideological conditions. Yet, they also present an opportunity to foster closeness in an increasingly individualized world, reconnecting our daily lives to broader political and ideological beliefs. What fascinates me is exploring how we create kinship and intimacy in a world that pulls us apart – one that demands constant flexibility, individualism, and competitiveness, prioritizing careers and personal success over social relationships and community. Is there, perhaps, a way to live together in such a world, without losing these essential connections?

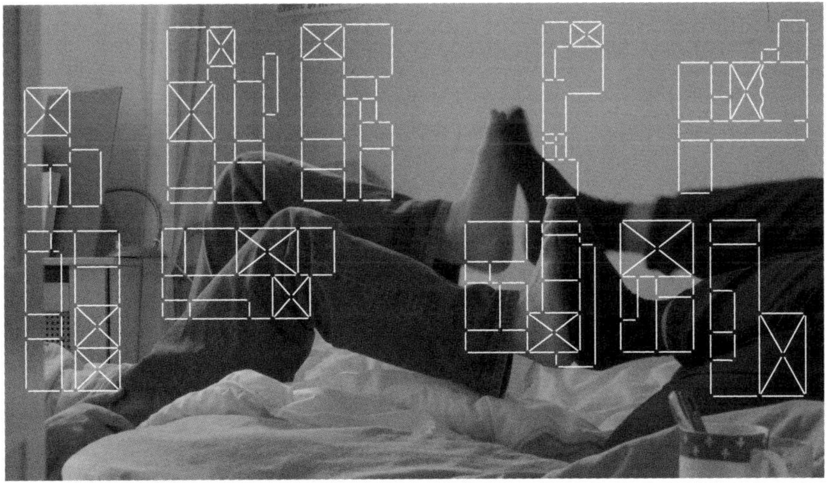

Susanna asked them to design a home

Can amicable feelings be an alternative form of love on which to base domestic life?

The kinship that can exist in a shared house is a special one; it is a necessary relationship, a forced one, but it's not related to blood ties, friendship, partnership, or common ideals. It is primarily a relationship rooted in the shared experience of living: domesticity intertwined with a sense of class and generational distress. This kinship is neither utopian nor entirely harmonious but rather broad and fluid, allowing space for ambiguity. These relationships might be described as "neotribal" bonds, shaped by shared goods and rituals, while the spaces themselves can be seen as "quasi-communes," where friendship becomes institutionalized within the domestic realm. Another lens through which to understand the shared household is Roland Barthes' concept of "idiorrhythm."[107] This term envisions a utopian form of living where individuals maintain their personal rhythms while coexisting in a community. According to Barthes, idiorrhythmic practices strike a balance between two extremes: complete withdrawal from society and compulsory interaction. Framing the shared household as idiorrhythmic reveals its potential as a response to individualism – one that simultaneously incorporates and transcends it.

Unlike Barthes' utopian idiorrhythm, however, the shared household is often far from ideal. Its inhabitants typically value independence and autonomy but are compelled to navigate interdependence. Yet these relationships – marked by a certain queerness and anarchic spirit – serve as bridges to a new kind of togetherness, one that redefines the boundaries of community in unexpected ways.

107 Roland Barthes, *How to Live Together: Novelistic Simulations of Some Everyday Spaces*, trans. Kate Briggs (New York: Columbia University Press, 2013). Lectures originally delivered at the Collège de France, 1976–77.

They asked me to design a house,

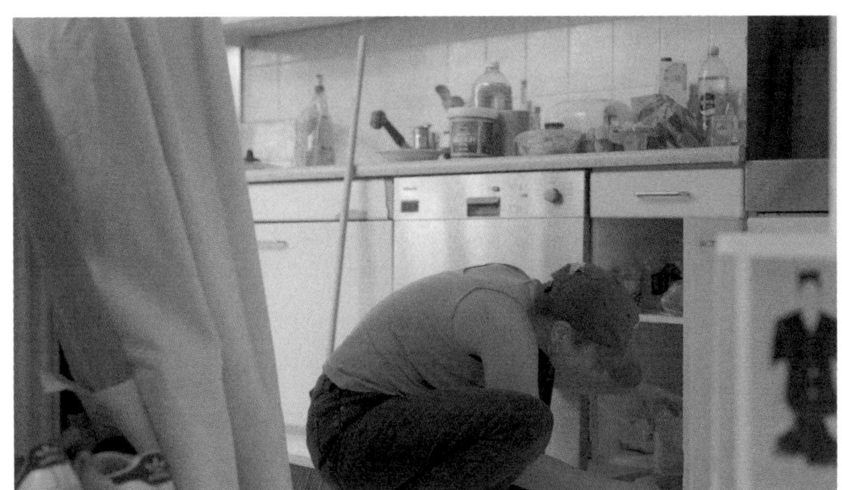

You buy paracetamol and make chicken broth when they are sick, they touch your shoulder when you cry.

Is all of this political?

Susanna asked them to design a home

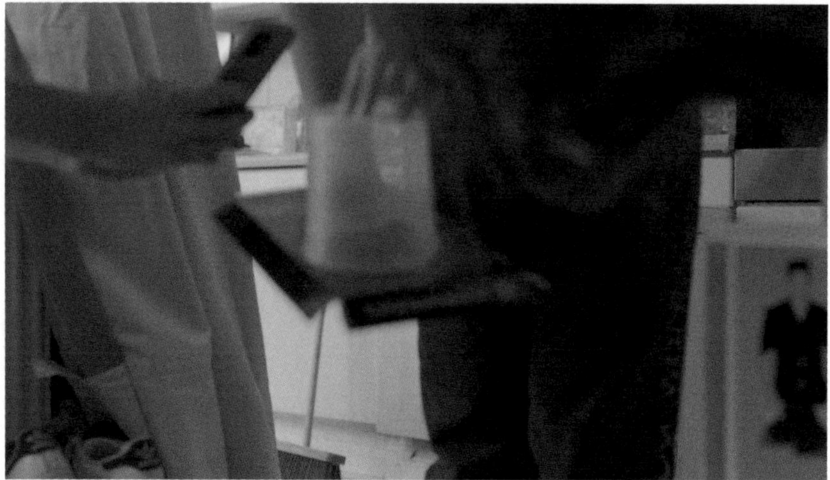

There is a sense of wonder in the traffic jam,
there is a sense of potentiality.

The experience of forced collectivity could maybe bring us to a valorization of reproductive work, collectivity, care, mutual support, and alternative kinds of ownership. Managing such a household requires trust, care, commitment, time, and energy – transforming living from a passive act into a profoundly political one.

The political structure of the shared household is usually based on assemblies and commonly agreed-upon rules. Other elements that can be found are schedules and group chats that regulate the common living, however, there are no norms on how a shared house should be structured, and a new equilibrium is found in each house. Analyzing our domestic spaces we might find ourselves wondering: How do we live together?

In exploring this question, it's worth reflecting on historical analogies between monarchy and the patriarchal nuclear family. Both structures centralize power in a single figure – the king or father – who dictates decisions, rules over others, and claims ownership. While contemporary systems may not directly replicate this patriarchal model, its echoes remain in our electoral democracies and organizational frameworks.

To push this speculative comparison further, imagine a society organized not around the traditional family model but the dynamics of a shared household. What new possibilities could arise from such a paradigm shift? Could we envision alternative ways of cohabitation and collaboration that move beyond hierarchical structures, creating more equitable and inclusive forms of living together?

They asked me to design a house,

Everybody is in their car again, looking ahead, everybody goes somewhere alnoe.

One final aspect of this kind of household is provisionality. While care and a sense of commonality can emerge in such spaces, they remain inherently temporary and precarious. This sense of impermanence is, I believe, beautifully encapsulated in Cortázar's story. In the seemingly endless traffic jam, life unfolds in a shared, collective rhythm – until, one morning, the standstill unexpectedly ends. While Dauphine is still asleep in the 404, the cars begin to move. Everyone rushes back to their vehicles. For a brief moment, Dauphine and the 404 exchange glances through their windows, but soon, differing speeds pull them apart. The 404, slower, falls behind. Helplessly, he watches Dauphine disappear into the crowd of cars ahead.
As he looks around, the faces and vehicles are no longer familiar. Strangers fill the space that once held a fragile community. Everyone is once again in their own car, looking forward, moving toward an unknown destination – alone.

For all previous images:
Still from video
installation, 2023.
Copyright: Susanna
Tomassini.

SUSANNA TOMASSINI is an Italian visual designer based in the Netherlands, holding a MA in Information Design from the DAE. With her practice she looks for new narratives around complex social and political topics, aiming for a deconstruction of apparently mundane subjects. Her approach is multidisciplinary, merging and alternating digital and printed media. Originating as a graphic designer, she is now exploring video as an artistic medium.

They asked me to design a house,

THROUGH THE DOOR

Non-Aspirational Kinship

Ramón Jiménez Cárdenas

During my Master's, in my twenties, I began to question whether I wanted to have children. At the same time, I started to wonder why this question felt so natural to me – especially as a body without a uterus. As I traced back this desire, I was confronted with the ideals of comfort that surrounded me, particularly the notion of a heteronormative relationship. The nuclear family, as a heteronormative kinship arrangement, maintains an apparatus of socio-ecological injustice that emerged in the era of settler coloniality in the Americas. Therefore, I wonder what it means to aspire to become a nuclear family, the same social unit that modern toxicity-making nations and economic systems depend on. To my understanding, this means that kinship itself – the way in which we articulate how we are tied to each other (the way we love and fuck!) – can become a form of resistance and a means to deeply alter the systems that control us. So, why not start there?

The nuclear family is defined by its overattachment to and dependency on "blood relatives." It distances itself from other social organizational forms, especially those involving reproductive labor: child-rearing and bearing, housework, elderly care, etc. This model perpetuates a culture of self-reliance, the foundation of neoliberalist economic systems where narratives of the self-made procreate. That is the reason why for so long the model of the nuclear family has been enforced (mostly through religious and biological institutionalization) by colonial states, which are apparatuses for endless growth.

Within the nuclear family, hierarchies that are imposed upon women and children are biologically reasoned. Gender, therefore, is constructed as a biological reality rather than a social performativity. The acceptance of biology as a socially anchored truth means that you must embrace your reproductivity and accept the intrinsic heteronormativity of the nuclear arrangement: Boys must become fathers and girls must become mothers. The heteronormative nature of the nuclear model itself ensures the continuation of the family regime over the generations. It can be considered a gift, even as the gift of life itself. To compensate for this gift, one must give back to the family: Turn parents into grandparents by following the other sex as a love object.[108]

108 Sara Ahmed, *Queer Phenomenology: Orientations, Objects, Others* (Durham, NC: Duke University Press, 2006), 85.

Therefore, marriage has been institutionalized (by church and state) to become more than merely a union of two. It is now a statute of numerous moral and legal benefits, economically incentivizing the "right kind of people" to reproduce. From the beginning of the colonization of the modern-day U.S. and Canada, Indigenous people were assimilated into the national body by being forced to adopt the nuclear family model. Institutions such as residential schools, churches, and missions were designed to "save the man and kill the Indian." Forced conversions to whiteness rampaged Indigenous territories.[109]

109 Kim TallBear, "Making Love and Relations Beyond Settler Sex and Family", in *Making Kin Not Population*, ed. Adele Clarke and Donna J. Haraway (Chicago: Prickly Paradigm Press, 2018), 163.

Large areas of indigenous land were dispossessed precisely through atomization of the collective and individualization. Indigenous kinship was abolished, and the extended family became legally non-existent. Moreover, kinship with the land was now a void concept within the colonial nation. By introducing the language needed to buy, sell, and profit, settler coloniality imposed a new economic regime where more-than-human bonds (kin with the land and its ecological rhythms), became an impossible pursuit. The curtailing of kin multiplicities and the separation of humans from nature enabled an epoch of enslaved human, animal, and plant life for extractivist purposes.

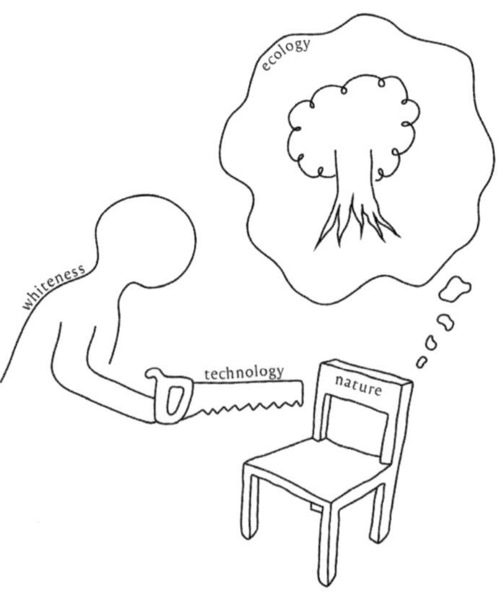

Figure 1
Ecology. Illustration, Ramón Jiménez Cárdenas, 2021. Copyright: Ramón Jiménez Cárdenas.

They asked me to design a house,

110 Donna J. Haraway, 'Making Kin in the Chthulucene: Reproducing Multispecies Justice", in *Making Kin Not Population*, ed. Adele Clarke and Donna J. Haraway (Chicago: Prickly Paradigm Press, 2018), 70-71.

Here, we can begin to identify the nuclear model as a set of values but more so begin to recognize it for its transparency. The political making of the nation can be theorized as colonial authorship: The body is the material, whiteness is the author, and transparency is its means. The outcomes are "the depletion of grasslands, forests, and soils, intensified mono-cropping and mining, rising carbon emissions, displacement of people and other critters from homelands [...] in the way of profit."[110]

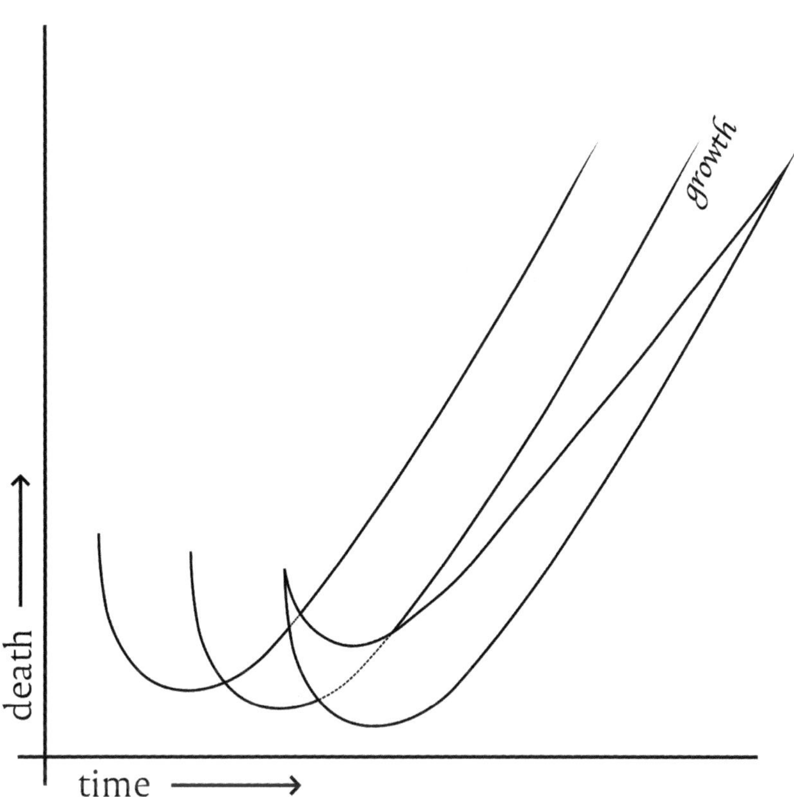

Figure 2
Nike curves. Illustration, Ramón Jiménez Cárdenas, 2021. Copyright: Ramón Jiménez Cárdenas.

Within this colonial apparatus, the medium of transparency makes the nation-state plausible. It helps formal and informal authorities, and social policing gestures to recognize those who have been incorporated into the national body and to marginalize those who resist. When whiteness stands in for the colonial political project that historically emerged notoriously at the same time the nuclear family did, transparency now succeeds it as a form of post-racial or multiracial whiteness. It stands in for an accord between subjectivity and ruling power and is not limited to white bodies.

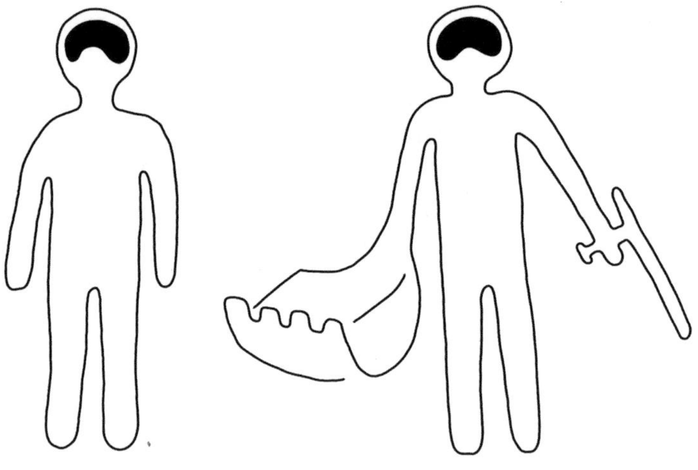

Figure 3
Unconsious. Illustration, Ramón Jiménez Cárdenas, 2021. Copyright: Ramón Jiménez Cárdenas.

I also question the role design holds in all of this. Infrastructure, transportation, four-door cars, highways, suburbanization, houses, kitchens, schools and education, health insurance, and even health itself, are all designed to fit the nuclear family. The overdesigned image of the family is part of an economizing network geared to picture all other settings in which people mix and live as aberrations. "Nurseries, children's homes, student residences, nursing homes, old people's homes, all in their different ways conjure up pictures of bleakness, deprivation, acceptable perhaps for daycare or for part of the year or a brief stage in life, but very much a pis aller to be resorted to only if normal family life cannot be provided."[111]

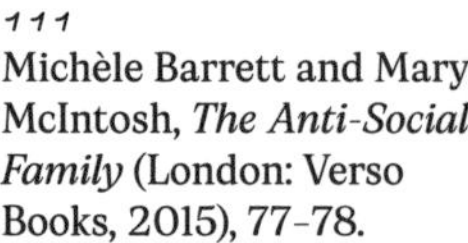

111
Michèle Barrett and Mary McIntosh, *The Anti-Social Family* (London: Verso Books, 2015), 77–78.

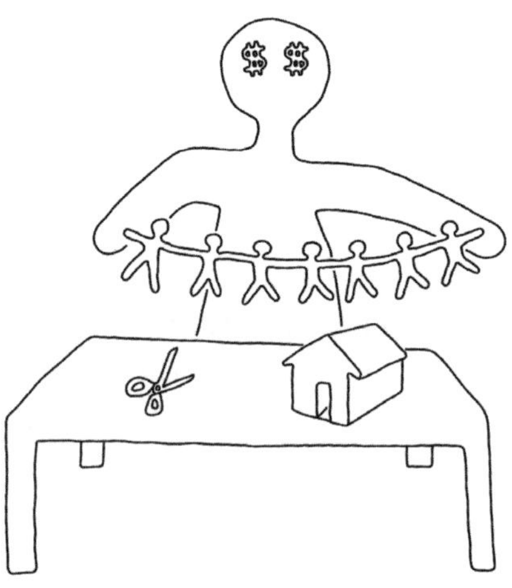

Figure 4
Paper people. Illustration, Ramón Jiménez Cárdenas, 2021. Copyright: Ramón Jiménez Cárdenas.

They asked me to design a house,

Countries like Denmark, Turkey, Japan, Taiwan, Hungary, and the U.S. cling to a low fertility narrative to counter dwindling populations of a particular ethnic/racial composition that are proclaimed as "demographic emergencies" of "not enough of the right kind of people." Their efforts range from financial incentives such as interest-free loans, tax cuts, and credit for couples, to setting up cabinet and ministerial positions to respond to the "fertility crisis." This is a commodification but more so an economization of morals and aesthetics, a fine-tuning of capitalist desires, and a policing of subjectivities that don't pursue the American Dream.

When we consider fertility as something that goes beyond the mere biological component and begin to involve the well-being and happiness of uncategorizable progeny, we start to acknowledge all oppressions as toxicities. Medical and judicial operations against reproductive, social, and environmental justice, institutionalized police brutality, family exclusive fertility clinics, systemic racism, coerced IUDs, oil spills, air pollution, and the enforcement of contraception as a legal measure against poverty; that's the real fertility crisis. These, and many other forms of mutilating body and land, make me wonder what it means to be fertile in an infertile environment. What does it mean – for human and non-human life – to be fertile while swimming in a toxic spill?
"The political world is hopelessly (and hopefully) intertwined with the natural world."[112] To that I would add: The personal is political and the political personal. Since the nuclear family is the ultimate goal of the transparent body (in the political regime as it is), I like to think of a form of making kin without predefined aspirations. Family not being the end goal but only our means for survival, where the sole practice of theorizing, making, and sustaining a "family" (call it what you want) becomes a reciprocal process between kinship and politics.

112 Bill McKibben, 'Racism, Police Violence, and the Climate Are Not Separate Issues', *The New Yorker*, 4 June 2020.

Figure 5
Author's sibling, Luca, taking a bath, 2016. Copyright: Ramón Jiménez Cárdenas.

Figure 6
Luca's drawing, 2021. Copyright: Luca López Cárdenas.

They asked me to design a house,

Ramón asked them to design a home

RAMÓN JIMÉNEZ CÁRDENAS (Oaxaca, Mexico) is an artist and curator based in Rotterdam. He works with and against modernity, mestizaje, and cultured nature. Drawing inspiration from autoethnographic research and found objects that develop into functional works, installations, or moments to share research. He is the curator of La Clínica, an artist-led artspace, and residency located in Oaxaca, Mexico.

They asked me to design a house,

THROUGH THE DOOR

Design Tools for Representation, Belonging, and Spatial Justice

Conversation with Setareh Noorani

ILARIA AND GEORGINA ✷ How did you start? How did you go from your studies to the direction you are undertaking now?

SETAREH ✷ If we want to make a significant change in how design can impact or work towards a more inclusive social environment, we have to think in a multidisciplinary way. And, a way that goes towards a radical imagination of our future. This, for me, is both the future that we aspire to have and, at the same time, the bare minimum we must demand. It has to inform the revolution that we have to carry out, but, meanwhile, also inform the reforms that we have to make in our current policies.
If I think back on how I started, during my time at the Architecture Department of the Delft University of Technology, I was involved in different student groups. I am indebted to my friends. Together, we discussed many things, focusing on how we felt about our education, whether the curriculum represented us, and the overarching issue of underrepresentation, which emerged as our main conclusion. At one point, I was in the Decolonizing Architecture working group, a Feminist working group, and I joined ARGUS – the student association of my Master's. At that point ARGUS was operating in a more traditional organizational form. Myself and friends, like Aska Welford, Willie Vogel, and Catherine Koekoek, decided that we wanted to organize in a more horizontal way, through affinity groups. These different organizational models and affinity groups were a rehearsal of how we could gather across different interests. This horizontal approach meant a lot, especially in how it facilitated efforts to communicate its importance to both teachers and students.
There was another fundamental point when Tomi Hilsee and María Novas put effort into organizing The Exhibition in the Corridor. This exhibition was a protest against the missing diversity of the (architect) portrait wall displayed as canon. At the end of the literal corridor, you also had a wall of names of star architects. On both the portrait wall and the wall of names, the majority of those represented were white males. I think that the protest efforts to position ourselves against this overwhelming dominance had a major influence on the projects I later developed.
At the same time, you still need to do these individual designing projects, group work, and write your thesis. It was during those moments (of theoretical study next to active collective practice) that I nurtured the interest in what is passed down to us by previous generations. The project that I graduated with was an embodied archive, in post-war/post-genocide Bosnia and Herzegovina. I tried to work with the notion of assemblage (from Deleuze and Guattari), and delved deeper into what it means to work through differences, viewing them as productive, aiming to create a setting for dialogue. That embodied archive can serve as a tool for dialogue, allowing us to rehearse the future by reflecting on what has been passed down from the past. The combination of activist work – and how I translate it into projects – informed how I positioned myself after graduating and influenced my work at the Nieuwe Instituut, and as

a designer. I am very interested in how to use architecture to stage dialogues, how to create a work informed by 'orientation', or how to create and wield tools as 'orientation devices'; I am borrowing this from Sara Ahmed. Thinking about tools, I'd like to offer the famous Audre Lorde quote:

"Those of us who stand outside the circle of this society's definition of acceptable women; those of us who have been forged in the crucibles of difference – those of us who are poor, who are lesbians, who are Black, who are older – know that survival is not an academic skill. It is learning how to take our differences and make them strengths. For the master's tools will never dismantle the master's house. They may allow us temporarily to beat him at his own game, but they will never enable us to bring about genuine change. And this fact is only threatening to those women who still define the master's house as their only source of support."

Here, she talks about survival not being an academic skill. I really think that survival is a skill that's transferred to us from other generations. So, we need to turn to our activist and feminist elders to learn these survival skills. I think the same goes for architecture. There's so much to learn from queer architects and women architects from older generations. They have learned skills that we can put to good use, if transferred. I think there were so many agents who were able to work together through their differences to negotiate different forms of house and city planning or policies. We need to communicate, intently and through generations, with each other in order to survive. This is a political project. I mention this in the Women in Architecture publication and several other papers: The knowledge transferred to us, both from our archival records and oral histories, can significantly inform our practice. These sources can shape future practice by broadening our understanding of how architecture can be created.

ILARIA ✷ How do we move from a space of survival to a space of belonging? How do you think the current architectural tools are trying to achieve that shift? Should discussions about belonging be part of the dialogue between designers and users?

SETAREH ✷ I think belonging is a form of survival. I also believe that survival skills teach us how to build relationships, foster community, and, as bell hooks describes, engage in the act of homemaking. Not only belonging or homemaking in a domestic space, but also as planetary survival with more-than-human agents.
In a project at Nieuwe Instituut, 'Collecting Otherwise', our Working Group currently talks about *hard tools* and *soft tools* (introduced by Harriet Rose Morley). Some of these soft tools are conversational skills or skills of transferring information. If I compare it to architecture, it may be the way you draw a plan or the way you conduct a user survey. Similarly, hard tools are found in different design stages. In the preliminary design stage, you have some hard tools like the plan you have to present. How do you make sure communication happens transparently? How do you communicate input from

They asked me to design a house,

the client back to the builder? Here, I refer to the Matrix Feminist Design Co-Operative. They have applied this, along with muf architecture/art: Instead of viewing the relationship between the client and yourself as purely economical, you collaborate on radical organizing. Many of these meetings are not only intended to discuss the design of the building but also to address their financial problems. You then try to incorporate this information into the program requirements. Another example is Burgerziekenhuis voor Vrouwen by Henriëtte van Eys, Luzia Hartsuyker, and others. For me, these cases are really inspiring. They're examples of realizing (note: as gerund, a non-finite action) a feminist utopia: Coming together to ensure space for women to work, for childcare, and for safe women's housing, while maintaining ethical representation on the boards of those organizing. Instilling in everyone the sense that they can take a pen, annotate on the same drawing, thereby taking agency in the design process.

Figure 1
Anne Thorne (Anne Thorne Architects) on Matrix Feminist Design Cooperative, during *Counter to Vital Feminist Pedagogies* at Nieuwe Instituut, in collaboration with gta archives ETH Zurich, 2023. Photo Credits and Copyright: Tomas Mutsaers.

ILARIA ✷ You talked about orientation objects. Can you talk about how in your work and experience, this can be applied to the way we design domestic spaces?

SETAREH ✷ I might start with a more recent example. There is the interior design for Buro Stedelijk that I have been working on together with Jelmer Teunissen. The brief was to deconstruct how an institution works, or what affords an institution to work, especially an art institution, and bring it back to designed tools. Buro Stedelijk, still located in the Stedelijk Museum in Amsterdam, needs specific tools and surfaces to deconstruct its most used type of space: the white cube. But how can one approach the deconstruction of the white cube? I see this being all about inhabitation, using specific devices to change our perspective on how we inhabit [art spaces]. And this can range from seating to lighting to surfaces to host dialogue. So, the table could be rescripted to be the floor, and vice versa, and I am considering the agency that should be granted to visitors as users, as well as the agency they, as clients, can take on in facilitating this.
Ultimately, what was presented was a skeletal structure – a framework that enables many other possibilities. It embodies flexibility, potential, and a sense of fluidity, qualities I believe are central to understanding the capacity of orientation devices. In the book *Queer Phenomenology,* Sara Ahmed notes that in landscape architecture, the term "desire lines" is used to describe unofficial paths - those marks left on the ground that show everyday comings and goings where people deviate

from the paths they are supposed to follow. So, I believe the initial interventions were intended to encourage desire lines because Buro Stedelijk didn't yet know how their space would be used. I found the idea of flexibility and fluidity – of movement and self-representation – really important. Regarding the agency of visitors, part of this skeletal structure functioned as a tool for collectively shaping manifestations within the space and intentions or ideas for further use. How is this space going to be used? How do we provide care for the space after the delivery date? How can others perceive that they are actively changing the space, and that this process is not solely defined by the architect's initial interpretation?

ILARIA ✷ How do you involve minorities in your exhibitions?

SETAREH ✷ At Nieuwe Instituut, we worked on an exhibition titled "Designing the Netherlands, in collaboration with CRa (the Board of Government Advisors)". A retrospective and, at the same time, a future projection of 100 years of future-thinking in the National Collection of Architecture and Urban Planning. Many of these architectural plans or urban designs were conceived with a specific urgency regarding the future in mind; urgencies that are specific to political power, positionality and ideology. How to select specific objects that help us decipher which urgent matters, in climate change, financialization, or housing, and emancipation have been addressed by designers and planners in the Netherlands? How do we ensure regional representation, when speaking about the national scale? Moreover, when we talk about the Netherlands, it's not just about the land in Europe; it once included Indonesia as well. The Kingdom of the Netherlands still has territories in the Caribbean. When working with collections for presentations, it's an ongoing task to deconstruct what 'Dutch' and 'Dutch design legacy' truly mean, so we can represent the diverse stories people refer to when they say 'Dutch.'

GEORGINA ✷ What is this archive that you are working on now at Nieuwe Instituut?

SETAREH ✷ I work as a researcher at the Research department. I am involved in various projects, and in most of them, I'm working toward creating space for spatial justice. I do this by exploring theoretical examples or academic knowledge, including Black critical studies, Black cultural traditions, as well as feminist and queer theories. And, of course, archival sciences. It's interesting to see where these worlds meet. When it comes to spatial justice, I am engaged in issues like housing justice, and creating space for the representation of Black bodies, women, queer individuals, and all those voices that continue to be marginalized. And that is partially fulfilled by engaging with the collection that we keep, the National Collection for Architecture and Urban Planning at the Nieuwe Instituut. My work with the collection is channeled through the "Collecting Otherwise" project. The project took the National Collection as a testing ground. We ask ourselves, with our colleagues of the Research and Collections

They asked me to design a house,

department, what we preserve and in what ways we do this. So, you have the "who" and "what" followed by the questions of creating and sustaining relevant design knowledge for generations to come: "how", "for whom", and "which themes?" Collecting Otherwise thus examines the representation of minority voices in our collection and how we can improve this. It explores how to organize dialogues around care and shared agency in archiving and collecting.

ILARIA ✷ Working on and with archives, do you see the archive process as an operative network or a productive way to create knowledge?

SETAREH ✷ I think it is both, really. And it is something we are trying to work on in "Collecting Otherwise." We are working with the principle of the Tool Shed, testing many things at the same time. With the Archival Care Rider, we suggest to co-produce certain elements of the archive with the donors, while researching their archive. Historical materials as sources for annotations, alongside newer, more speculative annotations, are integrated into another tool called the Asterisk. Archives, especially architecture archives, contain many documents that hint at solid outcome or singular truths, but remain fundamentally a collective, collated body of work. I think an archive is also full of different interpretations that need to be challenged by activating them, making them dialogue with the contemporary. I think this contemporary approach to archive as something that is not fixed, but something that can be revisited, is a very

Figure 2
Collecting Otherwise: Building HERitage. 2021. Thursday Night Live! at Nieuwe Instituut. Photo Credits and Copyright: Simaa Al Saig.

meaningful way of working. It hands us the tools to approach the future with a bigger sense of freedom. Returning to the archive in search of a specific approach to a contemporary urgency, I believe, is a more productive way of working than revisiting the archive merely to extract canonical examples.

ILARIA ✷ Do you think in architectural education, archives, and case studies are introduced to develop tools for the future design of our living environments or are they still used to create standards?

SETAREH ✷ Yes, that's what I was taught and it was really not long ago. Of course, you need to know certain references and examples. They say you need to build a reference library in your head. But for me, this was the most tedious work; to learn all these projects with all the specific amounts and numbers attached to them; amount of residents, year of construction, and so on. It was so tedious because I didn't know what it could mean for my work. That's a mistake that has been made in curricula

and I think reference libraries can change.
You can also use your own experience.
I think the usage of references is closely interconnected with the network in which we operate. I believe education can do much better in introducing us to a variety of references, seeing clients as producing agents of these references.
That's the problem I had in my Bachelor's. There was a homogeneous teacher body, so they ended up providing me with a specific set of references that, once again, I didn't particularly relate to. It should have been more diverse and multidisciplinary.

They asked me to design a house,

foto: Edwin Boering

Luzia Hartsuyker, architect, en de Koordinatiegroep

11

Figure *3*
Luzia Hartsuyker, architect, and the coordination group in "Inspiratie en een lange adem: het projekt burgerziekenhuis voor vrouwen, nu en straks", 1988. Archive Vrouwen Bouwen Wonen, L. Tummers. Collection Nieuwe Instituut/ VBWO, 192.3. Photo Credits and Copyright: Edwin Boering.

Figure *4*
Installation view *Designing the Netherlands*, 2024. Photo Credits: Petra van der Ree. Copyright: Nieuwe Instituut.

Figure *5*
Buro Stedelijk, design Setareh Noorani and Jelmer Teunissen, 2023. Photo Credits and Copyright: Tom Philip Janssen.

SETAREH NOORANI is an architect, researcher and curator at Nieuwe Instituut, and an independent artist. Noorani's spatial and architectural designs emphasise her ongoing research into (institutional) spaces for collective inhabitation and appropriation, centering undernarrated voices. The designed spaces challenge contemporary value systems connected to art/architectural production, and employ a distinct visual language that is counter-'white cube'. Setareh Noorani's current (curatorial) research at the Nieuwe Instituut (Rotterdam, NL) focuses on the paradigm-shifting notions of decoloniality, feminisms, and non-institutional and collective representations in contemporary architecture, its heritage and future scenarios.

They asked me to design a house,

THROUGH THE DOOR

They Craft a Bed for Marriage, I Design a Bed for Desire

Rising Lai

The bed is where we begin our lives and days, as well as where we end them. In Taiwanese culture, the bed is also where a marriage begins but (supposedly) has no end. 紅眠床 (âng-bîn-tshn̂g) or "Red Sleep Bed" – "Red Sleeping Bed" in English – is a constructive and materialistic form of the concept of home, family value, and traditional marriage in Taiwan, which is full of linguistic, artistic, and contextual meanings. Homophony across languages due to multilingualism, transnational artistic style due to colonization, and craftsmanship across geography due to social change are vividly demonstrated in this artifact. However, although the "Red Sleeping Bed" is diverse in expression, it inherited the traditional ideology of gender roles, patriarchy, and heteronormativity. As a wedding gift from the family, the wooden pieces (雕板) and drawings inlaid in the bed frame were the visualizations of wishes and expectations for the couple. The carved decoration emphasizes the importance of reproduction and filial piety, making this artifact consolidate the unequal heaviness of family duty. For example, 龍鳳呈祥 ("Husband and wife living in harmony"), 望子成龍 ("Witness your son mature and become successful"), and 多子多孫 ("Have a lot of sons and grandsons"). The woman is asked to be a (good) wife, mother, and labor but not herself.

紅 (âng) is pronounced similarly to the word 安 (an) in Taiwanese Hokkien. Therefore, "Red Sleeping Bed" sounds like "Safe Sleeping Bed," which gives the impression of reliability. The bed was initially designed to represent an ideal marriage. However, in the past, that meant being completely devoted to the husband's family as a woman. In Confucianism, we believe marriage is the cornerstone of society in which strict gender roles are applied. Yet, society has changed, and such attitudes have become more relaxed. Nowadays, diversity and inclusion are the new consensus. The "Red Sleeping Bed" demonstrated how a woman's independent identity disappeared after marriage, but how would it be shaped in the modern context? What if craft-making is centered on non-binary gender and/or non-heterosexuality? As a queer, I am curious about how a shift in mindset would alter the creation, while traditional craftsmanship is still practiced. What methods can be employed for material queer expression? The bed is supposed to be a safe place, as its name suggests. Therefore, I took on a journey to recontextualize a safe place for "ideal" marriage representation in the form of a traditional artifact. I visited five woodcraft masters - 洪耀輝 (Âng iāu hui), 黃裕凰 (N̂g jū hông), 侯瑞成 (Hâu suī sîng), 黃希宸 (Huáng Si Chén), and 石佳蕙 (Shíh Jia Hueì), who are life-long artisans skilled in traditional wood carving, religious furniture, and contemporary art. By conversing with the masters, I explored and gained insights into the possibilities of queering the "Red Sleeping Bed."

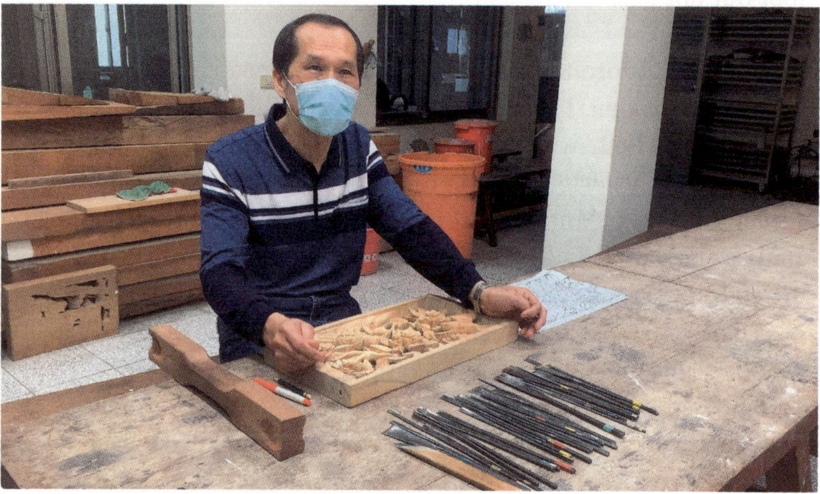

Figure 1–2
Visiting artisans skilled in traditional wood carving, religious furniture, and contemporary art, 2022. Photo Credits and Copyright: Rising Lai.

They asked me to design a house,

Master Âng is a national treasure of traditional woodcarvers in Taiwan. Over the course of his 40-year career, he has participated in numerous temple construction and conservation works as a woodcarver. He also teaches to pass down the techniques at the National Taiwan University of Arts. From his apprenticeship at an early age to becoming the most respected traditional woodcarver in Taiwan, Master Âng shared his experience in this life-long dedication to craft with me. He enlightened me with his modest attitude and the spirit of "being traditional" - a classic personality of old-generation Taiwanese that I can relate to. "What is considered a good work?" I asked him. "A work you devote yourself to," he answered.

Master N̂g is Taiwan's first and only female heir of traditional religious furniture artisans. She experienced people's doubts in this male-dominated industry and had to fight for acceptance. But eventually, she earned the respect and recognition she deserved. After 出師 (tshut-sai), which means completing the apprenticeship and being a master, she actively innovates the craft. She combines contemporary and feminine visual styles into furniture-making but always follows Taoism rituals and rules. She emphasized the importance of staying in awe of deities: "These rituals are irreplaceable," she told me. "They are part of our tradition and culture."

Mater Hâu, like Master Âng, has worked on numerous temple constructions. What's different is his trajectory. Between 1959 and 1972, the ROC government (before democratization) adopted laissez-faire policies to attract developed countries to invest in Taiwan. As a result, Taiwan became the primary out-sourcing manufacturing center of the USA and Japan. Back then, Mater Hâu worked in a Japanese-owned factory as a woodcarver, producing standardized and commercialized works that were later exported to Japan. Mater Hâu has rich knowledge and experience in "artistic craftsmanship" and "industrial craftsmanship." He explained their similarities and differences, and concluded that "the way you process and structure a work is important."

Artisan Huáng, mentored by Master Âng and Hâu while in university, is a wood carving artist/artisan based in Sam-kiap-khu, which is famous for its history of craft. Huáng and his peers are the new generation of traditional art. They have higher education and obtained the skills in university instead of the classical apprenticeship path like their mentors. To Huáng, the practice is more diverse, ranging from art pieces to goods. He explained how to reference folklore and literature, transcending them into subtle, symbolic carvings: "You can use the same visualizing methods as the masters to display the queer stories you want to tell," he suggested.

Artist Shíh came from a traditional artisan family. Her father, 石振雄 (Shíh Jhèn Syóng), is a highly respected wood figure sculptor, and her mother is a painter of 傳統彩繪 (traditional decorative painting). Unlike her siblings, who continue on the path of conventional wood carving, Shíh Jia Hueì is moving towards fine art, after being trained by her dad and university mentor – 吉田敦 (Atsushi Yoshida), a Japanese artist/sculptor resided in Taiwan. She shared her thoughts about her learning process and inspiration in wood carving: "You express your passion and reflection in the chosen theme, resonating with the audience."

This enlightening and inspirational journey to find the root of making, opens up the discussion of "queer" intervention: How can tradition and queerness coexist in design attitude, belief, structure, sourcing, and expression? Reflecting on all the aspects of making, I realize that the intersection of tradition and queerness is not controversial. Tradition, in fact, provides the fundamental means and forms for interpreting queerness in practice. Ultimately, I applied the instruction and guidance from the custom, building a redesigned artifact titled "Crafting Desire."

Figure 3
Red Sleeping Bed is placed in the household registration office in modern days for the newlywed couple to take a picture.
Source: 郭顏慧,2015.
Copyright: The Liberty Times 自由時報

Figure 4
Red Sleeping Bed placed in the household of a lifelong partner in the previous generation.
Year: unkown. Source: family archive.
Copyright: unkown.

They asked me to design a house,

The material world offers a vital framework for the formation of collective memory. In this regard, artifacts can be seen as containers of concepts, especially in light of the fact that what we think reflects the objects we make, choose, and use. In other words, our mind is inseparable from objects. "Crafting Desire" is more of a start than a result. By witnessing the transformation of the old "Red Sleeping Bed," this project changes how we engage with spatial, emotional, material, sexual, and territorial aspects of everyday reality. The bed becomes a place of belonging, demonstrating love and queerness – a bed for desire.

Figure 5
"Crafting Desire," an exhibition of the re-design queering Red Sleeping Bed, produced by Rising Lai, 2022. Photo Credits: Helena Roig. Copyright: Rising Lai.

RISING LAI is an artistic researcher and critical designer who uncovers the stories behind objects. From industrial products to cultural artifacts, Rising explores the complexity of human creation and curates these narratives in a communicative manner. Through design, their works research, contextualise, and speculate on the relationships among society, individuals, and material culture.

They asked me to design a house,

THROUGH THE DOOR

The Living Memory of Displacement

Ilaria Palmieri

I hold a bachelor's degree in interior design and a master's in interior architecture – qualifications that often lead people to view me as someone who shapes interior worlds, primarily in relation to the idea of home. To them, I am the one who selects furniture, colors, lighting, and materials – the elements they believe define a "designed" home. This perception is rooted in a static, normative understanding of the discipline – one that assigns fixed functions to spaces and limits design to fulfilling predefined roles. Even my own education in the spatial field nearly confined me to this conventional framework: designing based on inherited knowledge rather than reimagining new possibilities.

I began to break free from this mindset in the summer of 2017 while volunteering at an asylum seeker center in Sicily, Italy. There, I came to understand that design's impact extends far beyond arranging rooms, calculating the number of toilets, or ensuring access to kitchen areas. I witnessed how displacement is often framed solely as a state of homelessness – defined by loss and passivity. As a result, design interventions in these contexts tend to treat refugees and migrants as passive recipients of aid, rather than as active participants in shaping their own environments. But what if we viewed displacement as a spatial practice – one in which displaced populations actively contribute to homemaking and urbanization, rather than simply being accommodated?[113]

[1]3
[Lu]ce Beeckmans, Ashika [Si]ngh, and Alessandra [Go]la, "Rethinking the [In]tersection of Home [an]d Displacement from [a] Spatial Perspective", [in] *Making Home(s) in [Di]splacement*, ed. Luce [Be]eckmans et al., [Cr]itical Reflections on a [Sp]atial Practice (Leuven: [Le]uven University Press, [2]022), 16.

This possibility often remains underexplored due to dominant narratives surrounding domestic architecture in migratory contexts – narratives shaped by conventions and rigid functions rather than lived experiences and adaptive practices. Reimagining these spaces, and the way we design them, requires moving beyond these limiting frameworks and embracing the complexity and agency inherent in displacement.

As a spatial designer with a deep passion for writing, I often find myself frustrated by the rigid conventions that dominate architectural research – conventions that rarely allow subjectivity to serve as a tool for challenging dominant narratives. Over the years, I have visited and studied the domestic spaces of displaced people, keeping journals filled with notes, impressions, and emotions. The decision to share these reflections is a recent one, inspired in part by reading Maretha Dreyer's *Years in the Waiting Room: A Feminist Ethnography of the Invisible Institutional Living Spaces of Forced Displacement.* Her work prompted me to consider how personal accounts and subjective experiences can contribute to a more nuanced understanding of displacement and spatial design.

"We reflect on our roles, on the impact of the research upon our personal and professional lives, on our relationships with participants, on our perception of the impact we may be making on their lives and on our negative and/or positive feelings about what is happening during the research process".[114] Reflecting on one's feelings and emotions within the private space of a journal can open pathways to new insights, enabling researchers to engage with their work in a more open and honest way. It allows them to acknowledge their biases, confront uncertainties, and embrace the subjectivity that inevitably shapes their perspectives. Conventional academic writing, however, often leaves little room for this kind of self-reflection, discouraging researchers from expressing or processing the emotions they experience while conducting their studies. This limitation can create a disconnect between the lived realities they encounter and the ways in which those realities are represented in scholarly discourse.[115] As Elizabeth Dauphinee reminds us, "What we end up doing is privately remembering, rather than publicly writing [such experiences] into our publications. This divides our experiences in the field into public and private and, quite predictably, results in a silencing of the private."[116]

Encountering those words felt like an invitation – an opportunity to share the emotions, thoughts, and observations I developed through my research in asylum seeker centers. This act of sharing became my way of questioning how knowledge about displacement and homemaking has been historically constructed. By embracing subjectivity, we can challenge the idealized notion of objectivity in design and begin to create alternative memories for these spaces. Of course, I do so from a position of privilege as a white Western woman with access to education. Yet, it is precisely

114
Kim Etherington, *Becoming a Reflexive Researcher: Using Our Selves in Research* (London: Jessica Kingsley Publishers, 2004), 127.

115
Maretha Dreyer, "Years in the Waiting Room: A Feminist Ethnography of the Invisible Institutional Living Spaces of Forced Displacement", in *Making Home(s) in Displacement*, ed. Luce Beeckmans et al., Critical Reflections on a Spatial Practice (Leuven; Leuven University Press, 2022), 203.

116
Elizabeth Dauphinee, "The Ethics of Autoethnography", *Review of International Studies* 36, no. 3 (2010): 805.

They asked me to design a house,

Figure 1
On things I have heard. Illustration, Ilaria Palmieri, 2022. Copyright: Ilaria Palmieri.

Figure 2
Pieces of memory and imagination. Part of my exhibition "To be a host in a hosting country. Hospitality as empowermnet in asylum-seeker centers" at Nieuwe Instituut, Rotterdam, 2024. Photo Credits: Giulia Menicucci. Copyright: Ilaria Palmieri.

through my experiences with displaced communities that I have become aware of how design reinforces biased logics. These biases are deeply rooted in the way design is historically taught – we are often encouraged to operate within its established memory rather than engage with its lived realities.

From my first visit to a reception center in Sicily, I was struck by the disconnect between institutional environments and the lived experiences of their inhabitants. The spaces felt standardized, dictated more by policies than by cultural practices or personal needs. Over time, I came to see how these environments reflect broader systems of exclusion, reducing displaced people to passive recipients of emergency-driven design. Yet, within these margins, resistance, creativity, and informal practices emerge – revealing alternative ways of shaping space and challenging conventional notions of design. These overlooked acts of adaptation offer valuable insights into how we might rethink spatial practices with greater sensitivity and inclusivity.

From the outside
you wouldn't be able to tell
this is a reception center.

From the inside
you wouldn't say this is a home.

From the outside
you would say the space
is pretty big.

From the inside
you would feel how empty it feels.

(From my journal during my first visit
at asylum-seeker centers in Sicily, Italy, Summer 2017)

They asked me to design a house,

That was my first time in a reception center, yet I had no idea how familiar the feelings I encountered that day would become. I remember standing in front of the entrance gate for a few moments, uncertain of what to do. Should I ring the bell? Who would answer? Whose space was I about to step into? Who should I greet first? Was I entering as a guest? Was this a home? Or would I feel like an intruder in someone else's space?

Scholars Brun and Fàbos describe the "interconnected and multidimensional implications of homemaking in circumstances of displacement,"[117] through the concepts of "home," "Home", and "HOME."[118]
"home" refers to the everyday practices that help transform spaces of displacement into significant kind of places:[119] Personalizing temporary shelters, establishing daily routines, or fostering social connections within neighborhoods, camps, or institutions supporting refugees and internally displaced people.
"Home" emerges in relation to the social and cultural representation of "values, traditions, memories and subjective feelings of home."[120]
"HOME" extends beyond a physical place – it is shaped by the political and historical forces that define how it is experienced, both by displaced populations and by those who impose exclusion, violence, or policy-driven solutions. It reveals how individuals conform to, negotiate, resist, or redefine the labels assigned to them – such as "refugee" or "IDP" (internally displaced people) – and how these classifications shape identity and belonging. At its core, "HOME" embodies the tension between the loss of a familiar space and the resilience required to reconstruct one's sense of self and place within the realities of displacement.[121]

In public discourse, the concept of home and homemaking is often invoked as "HOME" to establish boundaries – defining who belongs and is welcome, and who is labeled as "foreign" or "alien," and therefore perceived as unwelcome.[122] The relationship between "HOME" and the ideals of "Home", and how they influence the spatial and temporal construction of a homeplace, can only be fully understood through "local empirical investigations."[123] By examining the material cultures and lived experiences of displacement, we can begin to recognize the potential for homemaking in even the most precarious conditions.

Ilaria asked them to design a home

117 Cathrine Brun and Anita Fábos, "Making Homes in Limbo? A Conceptual Framework", *Refuge* 31 (2 April 2015): 12–13.

118 Ibid.

119 Ibid.

120 Ibid.

121 Ibid.

122 Ashika Singh, "Towards Dwelling in Spaces of Inhospitality: A Phenomenological Exploration of Home in Nahr Al-Barid", in *Making Home(s) in Displacement*, ed. Ashika Singh et al., Critical Reflections on a Spatial Practice (Leueven: Leuven University Press, 2022), 67.

123 Ibid.

Bodies occupying beds
because occupying time seems impossible.

Trucks delivering food cooked elsewhere
because space is formed by policies rather than cultures.

Inside, standardization.
Outside, property questions.

One white wall left for us to express our struggles.
Yes, also mine.

(From my journal during my first visit
at asylum-seeker centers in Sicily, Italy, Summer 2017)

Years after those weeks in the reception center in Sicily, I found myself returning to similar spaces – reception centers, asylum seeker facilities, and refugee camps. These environments became central to my research, revealing the constraints of conventional thinking and the limitations of emergency-driven approaches in spatial design. In these spaces, political and cultural systems not only produce displacement but also dictate how displaced individuals navigate their circumstances, adapt, and attempt to rebuild their lives. Discussions on migration often take place at the scale of the nation or continent, yet the everyday realities of migrants unfold in the spaces where they seek shelter, work, and a sense of home. These are the places where they confront and negotiate state legal mechanisms and the exclusionary forces that accompany them. As a result, within the context of forced migration, home is often understood less as a fixed physical location or territorial connection and more as an emotional and relational experience – one shaped by resilience, adaptation, and the struggle for belonging.[124]

124 Brun and Fábos, "Making Homes in Limbo?", 8.

They asked me to design a house,

Figure 3
On things I have heard. Illustration, Ilaria Palmieri, 2024. Copyright: Ilaria Palmieri.

The domestic is a historically contingent constellation of references shaped by media representations, social norms, and personal experiences. While for some, the familiar markers of domesticity evoke a sense of safety and belonging, for others, they serve as reminders of trauma – often stemming from the very failure of domestic spaces to meet normative expectations or provide the protection and comfort they are presumed to offer.[125] This complexity demands a deeper reflection on the practice of homemaking in displacement – one that is shaped by the socio-cultural, political, and economic backgrounds of the homemakers themselves. It is a process influenced by a multitude of intersecting forces, including temporal dynamics, economic conditions, political structures, and spatial constraints, all of which collectively define the possibilities and limitations of creating a sense of home in exile.[126]

125 Nicholas Korody, "Intimate Distance: The Technosexual Architecture of Camming", *E-Flux* (blog), October 2019, https://www.e-flux.com/architecture/positions/280819/intimate-distance-the-technosexual-architecture-of-camming/.

126 Beeckmans, Singh, and Gola, "Rethinking the Intersection," 14.

Ilaria asked them to design a home

Can we talk about hospitality
in the absence of personal property?

How can we redefine hospitality
to view the host not just as an individual
but as a representation of territorial or national power?

How does the language of hospitality
obscure the power dynamics and violence
embedded in deciding who is allowed
to belong and who is excluded?

How can we recognize and challenge
the exclusivity inherent in hospitality practices?[127]

(From my journal during a research purpose visit at asylum-seeker centers, The Netherlands, 2022)

I do not see myself through the lens of those who, at the beginning of this text, defined me by their expectations. Instead, I have chosen to navigate the design of interior worlds as a means to expand the notion of home – conceiving it as a dynamic, multi-scalar entity rather than a fixed construct. My words, journal, and experiences – together with those of the many people I have met – made clear to me the need to rethink how memory informs the design of living spaces in displacement. This process must involve the creation of a historical memory of these spaces – acknowledging their past, their endurance, and their ongoing transformation. As Alessandro Petti and Sandi Hilal of DAAR suggest,[128] if we recognize refugee camps as having their own history, we can move beyond viewing them solely as sites of systemic estrangement. Instead, we

127 This series of thoughts emerged after a visit in a reception center when reading "On Solidarity, Community and Landscape," a conversation between Irene de Craen and Merve Bedir published in *Errant Journal States of Statelessness*, Issues 4, 2022.

128 Alessandro Petti, "Refugee Heritage. The Architecture of Exile IV. B", *E-Flux* (blog), February 2017, https://www.e-flux.com/architecture/refugee-heritage/99756/the-architecture-of-exile-iv-b/.

They asked me to design a house,

can understand them as spaces of significant activity – not only centered on survival but also on the continuous efforts to rebuild lives, assert agency, and claim legitimacy. Such endeavors, which can be viewed as various "microtechniques of lived experience,"[129] create *new* opportunities for establishing homes in contexts where the ideal of home and the process of homemaking are not easily accessible.[130]

Thus, while constructing a historical memory of these spaces is crucial, it is equally important to cultivate an operative memory – one that situates the concept of home within a broader web of places and contexts. Home is not always tied to a singular location; rather, it can emerge through a network of evolving and contested spaces. Embracing this perspective in design requires a commitment to intersectionality and subjectivity, ensuring that the realities of those inhabiting displacement are acknowledged.

Bringing forward my perspective as someone with the privilege and platform to amplify these voices, I am "constantly unlearning the impulse to create that we have inherited from our modern-driven design education. We embrace discomfort, moving forward with small steps and gestures, in a continuous process of imagining and enacting transformation."[131] By centering subjectivity and lived experience, design has the capacity to challenge oppressive narratives, forge new spatial memories, and reconceptualize homemaking as an act of resilience and agency.

129
Mariana Ortega, In-Between: *Latina Feminist Phenomenology, Multiplicity, and the Self* (State University of New York Press, 2016), 206.

130
Singh, 'Towards Dwelling in Spaces of Inhospitality', 77.

131
Griselda Flesler, Anja Neidhardt, and Maya Ober, "NOT A TOOLKIT. A Conversation on the Discomfort of Feminist Design Pedagogy"", in *Design Struggles. Intersecting Histories, Pedagogies, and Perspectives*, ed. Claudia Mareis and Nina Paim (Amsterdam: Valiz, with Swiss Design Network SDN, 2021), 207.

ILARIA PALMIERI is a spatial designer and interdisciplinary researcher working at the intersection of migration, dwelling practices, and participatory spatial politics. Her practice uses architectural analysis, ethnography, and participatory mapping to highlight migrant agency in their living environments and to translate these findings into housing policy. Her work has been exhibited at the Nieuwe Instituut in Rotterdam, Dutch Design Week, and the *What Makes a Home* Demo Days in Eindhoven, among others. Ilaria co-founded the research and design duo Common Ground Practice, which focuses on creating safe spaces for marginalized communities and fostering new, dominant memories within spatial practices. She is part of *Tre Sequenze*, an online Italian magazine dedicated to spatial culture.

They asked me to design a house,

Part Two
Exercises

Workshops as a Form of (Design) Resistance

Cecilia Casabona
Ilaria Palmieri
Georgina Pantazopoulou

INTRODUCTION

This contribution highlights four workshop series organized and hosted by Common Ground Practice between 2023 and 2024. While the organization continues to facilitate workshops focused on the theme of home and domestic environments, this text specifically emphasizes those series that played a pivotal role in shaping the development of this publication.

During our Master's studies, where we first met, particularly in relation to our graduation projects, we both explored and experimented with various workshop formats. These experiences were crucial in amplifying diverse voices within the discourse surrounding home, allowing us to collaborate and draw inspiration from one another. After founding Common Ground Practice following our graduation, we extended our workshop approach beyond the academic environment. Workshops became a platform not only for testing new ideas and exploring innovative tools and methods in research and design but also as a valuable feedback mechanism. They foster deeper connections between us and the participants, as well as among the participants themselves, promoting dialogue and collective learning.

We continue to work within the framework of workshops because they allow us to facilitate discussions on domestic environments across a variety of contexts. These sessions provide valuable insights that enrich our understanding and approach. The spontaneity that characterizes our workshops has been key in challenging the conventional notion that the design of a "home" should be solely the responsibility of architects or designers.

This collective approach – shaped by the relationships formed among participants, the conversations sparked, and the fresh perspectives introduced – has deeply influenced our reflections on our roles as designers and architects. It has also been immensely rewarding to witness the richness and mutual learning that emerge from these interactions. Through this iterative process, we continually build on the insights gathered from each session, using them to inform future workshops and to shape our practice as architects and designers.

MOMENTS OF FAMILIARITY

Moments of Familiarity, How to Create Anew? and *Home: A Site of Resilience* explores the deep connections individuals have with what we once called "home." These workshops are designed to empower participants to reconsider the complex relationships between themselves and their surroundings – encompassing not only physical spaces and objects but also the people, as well as sensory experiences such as sounds, smells, and light, which all contribute to our understanding of domesticity. Through simple exercises, the workshops create a space to reflect on what intimacy means, how it can be unraveled, and its profound importance in everyday life – even in the context of survival amidst restrictions, controls, and binary behaviors.

With the idea of engaging in a workshop format on the topic of domesticity within the precarious and uncertain living conditions of Asylum Seekers' Centers, we held several meetings with Stichting de Vrolijkheid. This organization is a network of artists, facilitators, volunteers, children, young people, and parents who run workshops and art projects at Asylum Seekers' Centers in the Netherlands. Together, we discussed our plans, considered possible scenarios, and formulated our approach. However, stepping into that space and meeting people directly felt as though everything had shifted.

Moments of Familiarity became a workshop we co-created with the participants, without a strict program or schedule. While we arrived with a few initial guidelines to structure the workshop, we found ourselves following rather than guiding, allowing the participants to shape the process.

We engaged in exchanges with young individuals aged fifteen to eighteen from Syria, Eritrea, and Ethiopia. As white, European expats in the Netherlands and not asylum seekers or refugees ourselves, we confronted those exchanges with a shared awareness of the differences in our experiences. We aimed to create a space comfortable enough to encourage expression, communication, and the possibility of reimagining *home.*

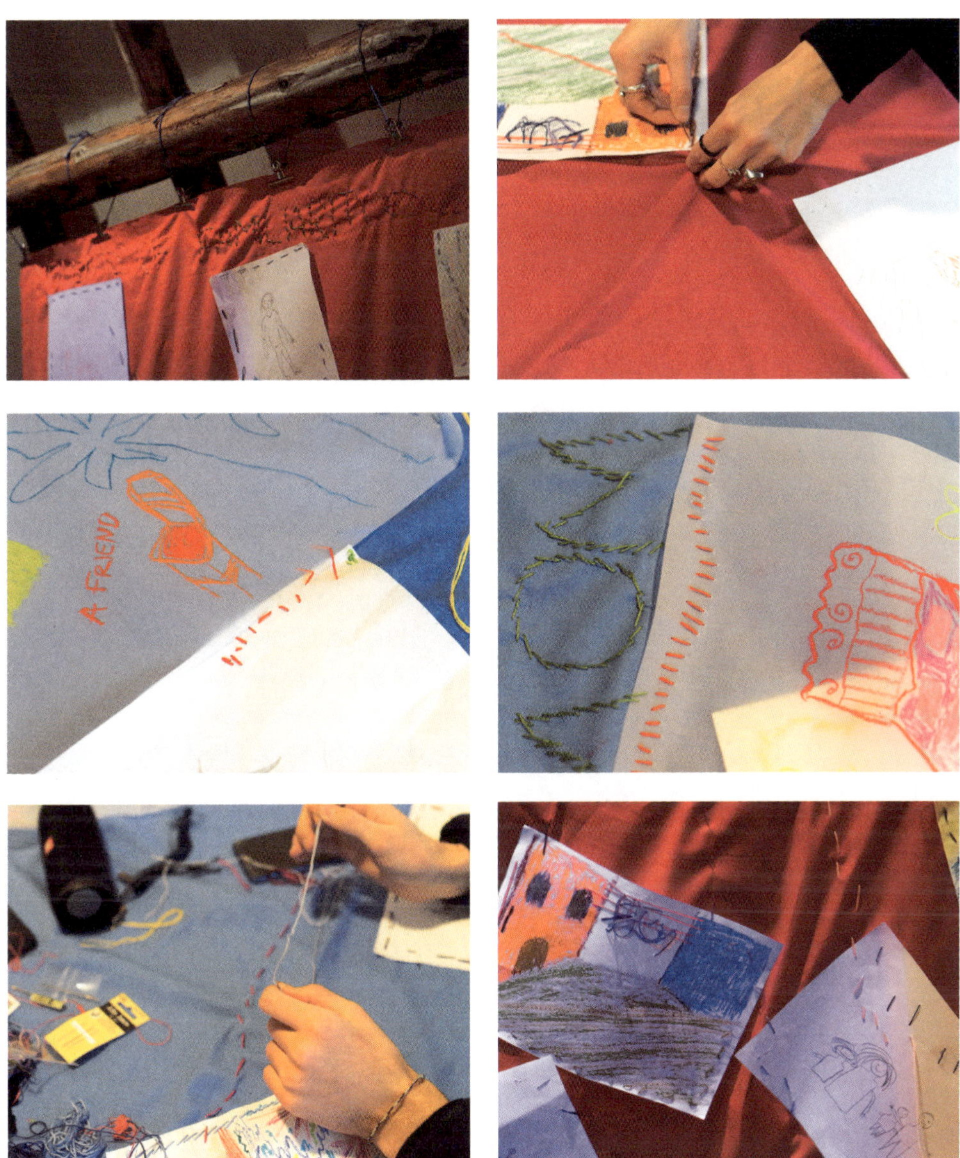

Images from the workshop, 2023. Photo Credits and Copyright: Ilaria Palmieri, Georgina Pantazopoulou.

MOMENTS OF FAMILIARITY

A game to share the ways we use our homes.
A game to interact in order to feel comfortable in our homes.
A game to create a temporary installation all together.
An installation to create community.
A live archive of what we mean by home.

With people with whom we
Did not share the same languages;
The same cultures;
The same experiences;
Yet we all shared an understanding of what we once called home.

And so,
there we were;
In that specific,
temporary space.

It was home,
but not home;

A place where everyone was constantly trying
to create a sense of domesticity.

Temporary.
Temporary.
Temporary.

We heard this word
– repeated in many languages –
countless times during our days there.

Suddenly, we felt at ease.

We began creating together through words and silence, through drawings and unspoken exchanges. Gestures.

Sometimes, we communicated only with our eyes;
Exploring what domesticity meant;
Past, present, and future.

Four sessions, January 2023
Divided in two sections
At the Asylum Seeker Center in Den Helder.

Two hours: We started by sharing our names, a piece of our backgrounds, and brief stories about home. Then, we gathered around a large table with paper, pencils, pastels, and a big piece of fabric. Together, we mapped familiar stories, crafting a shared map we then placed in the corner of what are defined as the "common areas" of these temporary spaces.
A reminder of what it feels like to be *at home.*
A possibility to engage with that memory.
An object that fosters community, for those who seek it.
An archive to trace the history of lives in temporary spaces.

Reflections

This collective creation brought moments of closeness, connecting diverse worlds through shared stories. It offered a glimpse of intimacy and it was a powerful exercise embodying both the influence and the potential for what might be possible.[132] *This participatory process allowed the knowledge produced through our collective exploration to become visible. It also challenged us to rethink traditional ideas of home and consider how temporary living spaces can better promote connection and belonging.*

132
bell hooks, *Teaching Critical Thinking*
(New York: Routledge, 2010).

HOW TO CREATE ANEW?

Since we moved to The Netherlands, we have been looking for community spaces – places to connect with different cultures, join community dinners, participate in book readings, and more. This search led us to De Voorkamer, a project and community space in Utrecht that fosters cultural exchange by welcoming people from diverse cultures and backgrounds. We began attending events and workshops there, and soon started to wonder: What if we explored the topic of domesticity in a workshop format within such a culturally rich space?

Inspired by the techniques the community was already familiar with – mostly lino printing workshops and embroidery sessions at the time – we started to consider how to integrate these approaches into our research. We mostly had a question in mind: How can we, as designers, pursue a design method that uncovers and activates voices and behaviours that are often unheard?

Following an invitation from De Voorkamer, we developed *How to Create Anew?*, a series of workshops aimed at exploring and sharing personal stories related to the domestic environment. Grounded in lived experiences, the workshop seeks to gather these stories and uncover new ways of sharing them, bringing designers and participants together to establish fresh principles for rethinking and redesigning domestic spaces. How can we make the design process more inclusive? How can we learn to interpret our domestic environments in new ways?

Using lino printing and embroidery techniques as a common visual language, the workshop brought to life multiple individual stories, each reimagining home environments – both physical and intangible – through the Dutch context and the diverse perspectives of participants' home countries.

Images from the workshop, 2023. Photo Credits, and Copyright: Ilaria Palmieri, Georgina Pantazopoulou.

Six sessions, April – May 2023.
Divided in 3 sections.

First two: *Are you a guest or a host?*
Do you feel like a guest or host?
Do you prefer to be a guest or a host?

These initial discussions opened a thoughtful examination of what it means to be either a guest or a host in various contexts. Participants shared personal stories first through words, and then began translating those stories into visual narratives using the lino technique.
A ten-metre piece of cotton fabric was laid on the table, ready to receive these narratives.
As the community map took shape, the space itself began to feel more familiar, reflecting insights into often unspoken aspects of belonging. These stories gradually articulated a shared sense of familiar contexts, revealing insights that, while rarely expressed, simply needed time and space to emerge.

Next two: *Gender roles and domesticity.*
How do we perceive gender within the home space?
Do we feel comfortable enough to express and connect within our own homes?

Participants explored how different cultural backgrounds shape our understanding of gender in private spaces. For many, especially those from Middle Eastern and African countries, stories of mothers emerged as central. Participants shared that in their cultures, the figure of the mother often symbolizes both strength and nurturing, embodying a powerful role as caregiver, listener, and advisor. Using lino printing, participants translated these stories and personal anecdotes into visual narratives, slowly weaving together a collective story that reimagined familiar gender dynamics anew.

Final two:

In the last two sessions, we shifted to embroidery, allowing participants to reflect on the previous themes, visually connecting the stories with one another. Familiar with this craft (most of them have followed lino and embroidery workshops at De Voorkamer before), many participants could express themselves in a more linear and contextual way, reinterpreting past discussions, acknowledging shared insights, and exploring ideas for the future.

We conducted these workshops hoping to replace extractive design practices with approaches that foster community ownership, recognition, and visibility.[133] Social worker Sophia Pekowsky assisted in guiding the lino workshops, helping to facilitate the process.

Reflections

Entering an existing community space familiar with lino and embroidery posed a unique challenge. Although participants were already used to these techniques, dedicating the six sessions to deeper thematic exploration required a shift in focus. Introducing ourselves and sharing personal stories first, proved helpful, encouraging openness and creating a warm, intimate setting. We were surprised by the shared values of inclusivity and equality, with discussions touching on intersectionality, feminism, and ways to recognize and challenge patriarchal dynamics, fostering a stronger sense of intimacy in home environments.

The culminating design – a long, printed and embroidered cotton tablecloth – was used to host a communal dinner in November 2023 for the opening of the collective exhibition Crafting in Community at De Voorkamer. This event invited participants to reflect, discuss, and create new memories around a shared table, bringing the workshop's journey to life in a tangible, interactive form.

133
Sasha Costanza-Chock, *Design Justice: Community-Led Practices to Build the Worlds We Need* (Cambridge, MA: MIT Press, 2020).

HOME: A SITE OF RESILIENCE

The workshops we hosted at the Asylum Seeker's Centers and at De Voorkamer let us realize how many different conversations, thoughts and inspirations can emerge when exploring the subject of domesticity while creating a collective piece within a specific context. This approach soon became a tool for us to design through research and, in turn, to research through design.

Willing to share our research methodologies and the trajectories we have been engaging with, we responded to an open call by Platform for Arts Research in Collaboration (PARC), an initiative of the Academy of Creative and Performing Arts of Leiden University (ACPA) and the University of the Arts The Hague, for the the Joint Research Day 2024.

We, once more, proposed a participatory workshop: *Home: A Site of Resilience.* Our proposal was selected and the workshop took place at the Royal Academy of Art The Hague on 22nd November 2024 and was open to the public with prior reservation. A total of twelve participants attended.

Designed in alignment with our previous workshops, this session aimed to research, explore, and share diverse understandings of domesticity through personal stories and lived experiences.
By gathering these narratives, the workshop encouraged designers and participants to collaboratively develop new principles for rethinking and redesigning domestic spaces. This time, we put a particular emphasis on using drawing as a communication tool.[134]

The workshop was structured into three exercises but maintained a flexible approach, allowing group dynamics to guide the flow and evolution of activities. The session lasted two hours.

134
See also Phyllis Birkby, "Herspace," in *Making Room: Women and Architecture*, *Heresies* 11, vol. 3, no. 3 (1981): 28–29

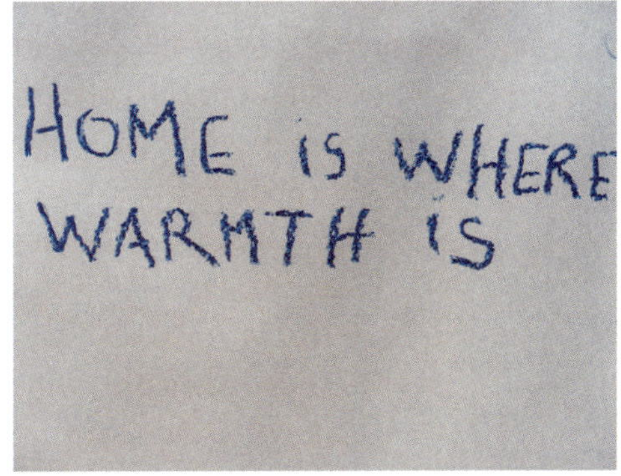

Images from the workshop, 2024. Photo Credits and Copyright: Georgina Pantazopoulou.

First Exercise:

We began with a warm introduction, allowing participants to get to know one another. This time, they were neither part of a pre-existing group nor members of a community. While some were familiar with the design field – marking the first time we engaged with such a group – others came with little or no prior experience. This mixture created an interesting and diverse approach to the workshop.

Using oil pastels and pencils on a big paper roll, participants were invited to draw and discuss fragments of their current domestic environments. These drawings captured rooms, objects, or moments significant to their daily lives and became the first element of the collective piece we were realizing.

The Ring Bell
The bookcase or the room of books
The kitchen – the light of the kitchen
A special sofa
A white space turning into something warmer (eventually)
Red, red objects – or maybe fire?
Purple creates intimacy
These conversations naturally led to reflective questions:

How did you choose your current place?
What brings you here?

Second Exercise: Thinking Otherwise

The large collage of stories and voices started to take shape. Some domestic experiences were recognized as familiar or similar by some of the participants. At this stage, we added a transparent foil over the canvas. Inspired by each other's stories, participants were invited to react to or intervene in one or more of the others' narratives, brainstorming and sketching potential changes or interventions for their chosen spaces.
The process resulted in a two-dimensional map that captured their collective aspirations. This exercise was not just about the tangible canvas but about weaving a shared understanding of domesticity through interaction and imagination.

Third Exercise: Manifesto

The final activity asked participants to reflect on their reimagined spaces and explore the relationships between their current and their envisioned environments. Each participant expressed their insights using their chosen medium – whether text, drawings, songs, or models. These personal manifestos became unique statements, shaped by the shared ideas and connections formed throughout the workshop.

Home is where warmth is
Girls in thve kitchen
Collective and personal intervening
Fly to arrive home – Let home transform
Grey but alive
Connecting with all senses

Reflections

The workshop took place in a familiar space for us – the Royal Academy of Art The Hague – where we both completed our Master's degrees. Open to all, the workshop attracted participants from outside the university environment, contrary to our initial expectations. While a few were familiar with architecture and design, many came from other arts-related fields, contributing a rich diversity of perspectives. This multi-layered group dynamic became a catalyst for exploration, as participants drew on their unique knowledge and experiences to discuss home, intimacy, and domesticity. Notably, most participants were already engaged with these themes in their personal or professional practices, making this session distinct from previous workshops.

One surprising observation was that all participants identified as female. While we believe this was coincidental, it brought a unique perspective to the discussion of home and domesticity. This dynamic also raised questions about how the process might have evolved with male perspectives included, reinforcing the persistent cliché of domesticity being closely associated with women.

Our hope is that throughout the workshop, imaginative ideas, thoughtful reflections, and creative expressions emerged, reaffirming the importance of collective exploration in rethinking the concept of home and domestic space.

Images from the workshop, 2023. Photo Credits and Copyright: Georgina Pantazopoulou.

FINISTERRAE – AN ODE TO THE TEMPORALITY OF FEELING AT HOME

Finisterrae is an experimental residency project located at the southern edge of Italy, in the Puglia region. We were invited by Martina Ciceri, a dear friend and architect, who had recently completed the renovation of a house her family had acquired in the small town of Presicce (LE).

Alongside five other designers from various disciplines, we became, in July 2023, the first to inhabit the renovated house as part of this experimental residency. We served as temporary inhabitants, experiencing the house as a home and using creative mediums to document our discoveries, impressions and connections with the local community.

During our week-long stay, we explored the spatial qualities of the house and immersed ourselves in the local area. This experience allowed us to create a dialogue between the house and its surroundings.
In the height of summer, amidst a major heatwave, the house became a refuge – a space for cooking, sleeping, dancing, discussing, reading, creating and relaxing.

The outcomes of the residency were showcased in an exhibition held within the house and open to the community of Presicce.

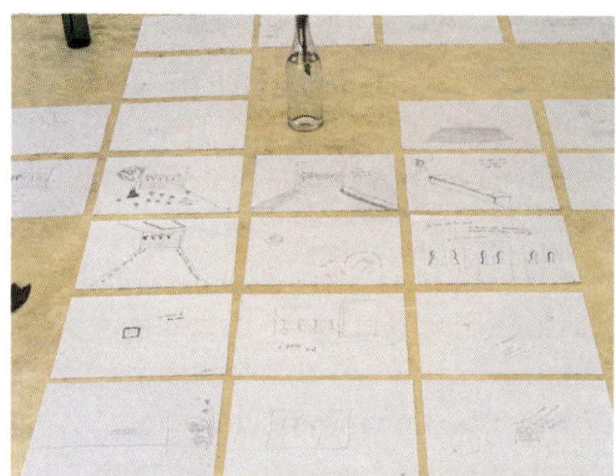

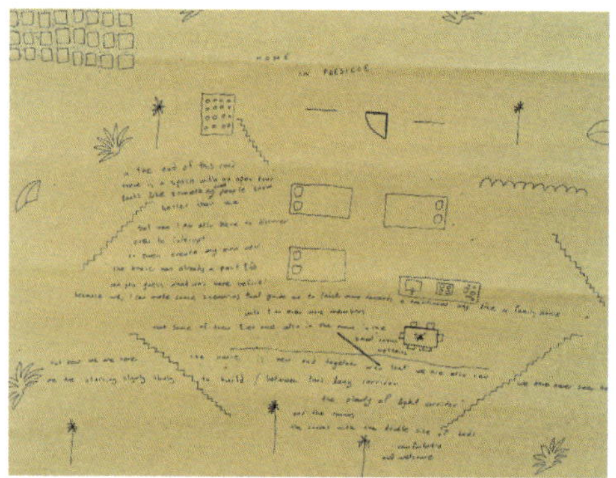

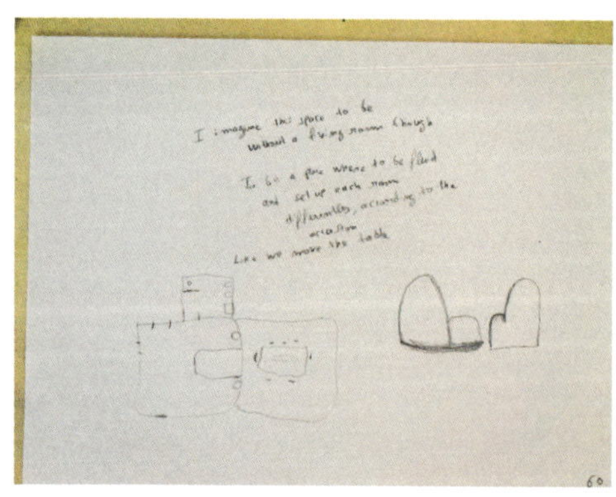

Images from the residency, 2023. Photo Credits and Copyright: Ilaria Palmieri, Georgina Pantazopoulou.

AN ODE TO THE TEMPORALITY OF FEELING AT HOME

At the end of this road,
there is a space with an open door.

Now I am here;
To discover;
To interrupt;
Or perhaps to create something new.

The house has lived before,
carrying a past life.
Can you guess what was here before?
I imagine its history, perhaps it was a
traditional family home,
with three or more family members.
Maybe some even lived in the small
room on the terrace.

And now, here we are.
Starting slowly, slowly.

The house is new to us;
And we are new to it.
Together, we begin to build something.
Through the long, light-filled corridor;
And the spacious, welcoming rooms
With beds large enough for comfort.

We have never been here before.
The house is becoming home.

We have already built a new kind of
domesticity, entirely rooted in community.
A community here to discover a few
magical things: The sun, the food, the
love.

Doors

Welcome to the south of Puglia.
Welcome to Salento.
Welcome to Presicce.

Together with the sun
Or even under its warmth.
We are here to read;
To speak;
To sleep;
And most certainly, to eat.

Pasta fresca with pomodoro
And fresh vegetables from the yard.
Shared with friends
And others;
Exploring this small,
or perhaps vast, amphitheatre.
A space designed to invite not only us
but also you;
To embark on a journey southward.

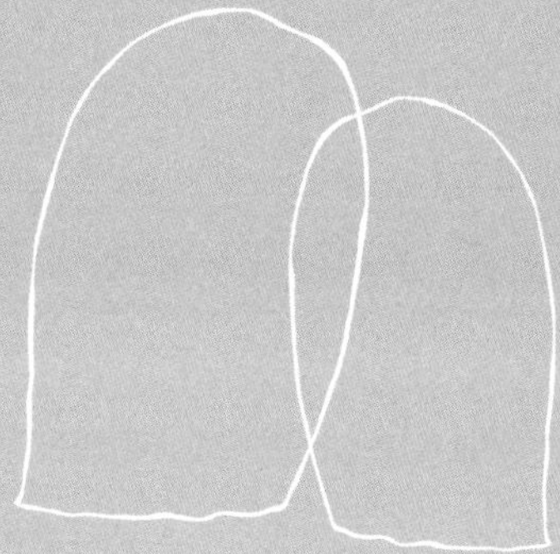

Floors

You can't tell where inside ends and
outside begins.
You're held steady
by the symmetry of shapes,
but something in you
craves to be swept away
by the organic freedom of light.
So, where do you go? What do you do?

Walls

There is a tightrope walker of Presicce,
but she is unusual: she comes out at
night, never walking in a straight line.
There's something fearless about her.
She disappears into the circular cracks
in the walls.
What's she doing there?
Why doesn't she ever come back to tell
us what she's seen?
Wait, there she is again.
I have to follow her.
See you later.

Gardens

I'm always expecting someone to ring
the doorbell.
But then I think: What door?
I imagine guests coming in through
the garden instead.
My eyes linger on the steps,
like they're the ones in
Piazza di Spagna, in my Rome,
alive with people.
I imagine figures emerging from the
broad leaves of towering plants rooted
in the red soil,
souls making their way toward us.
I'd like to think of them as tightrope
walkers,
but deep down, I know the truth:
Only those who live in this house are
tightrope walkers.
So, what about everyone else?
They're just passing through.
They're like owls.
Owls come and go,
but I imagine their passage
is always open.
That's the thing with owls: They take
paths the tightrope walkers never use.
I can guess where they're going;
But where they've come from, that's
still a mystery.

Bodies

In this story, we've crossed paths with
light, shapes, tightrope walkers, owls,
geometries, plants, and streets.
They make up the population of 62
Via XXI Aprile, Presicce (LE), Italy.
And then there's us,
trying to tell you
what it means to live here,
to share this space with them.

Exercises

In collaboration with
Cecilia Casabona

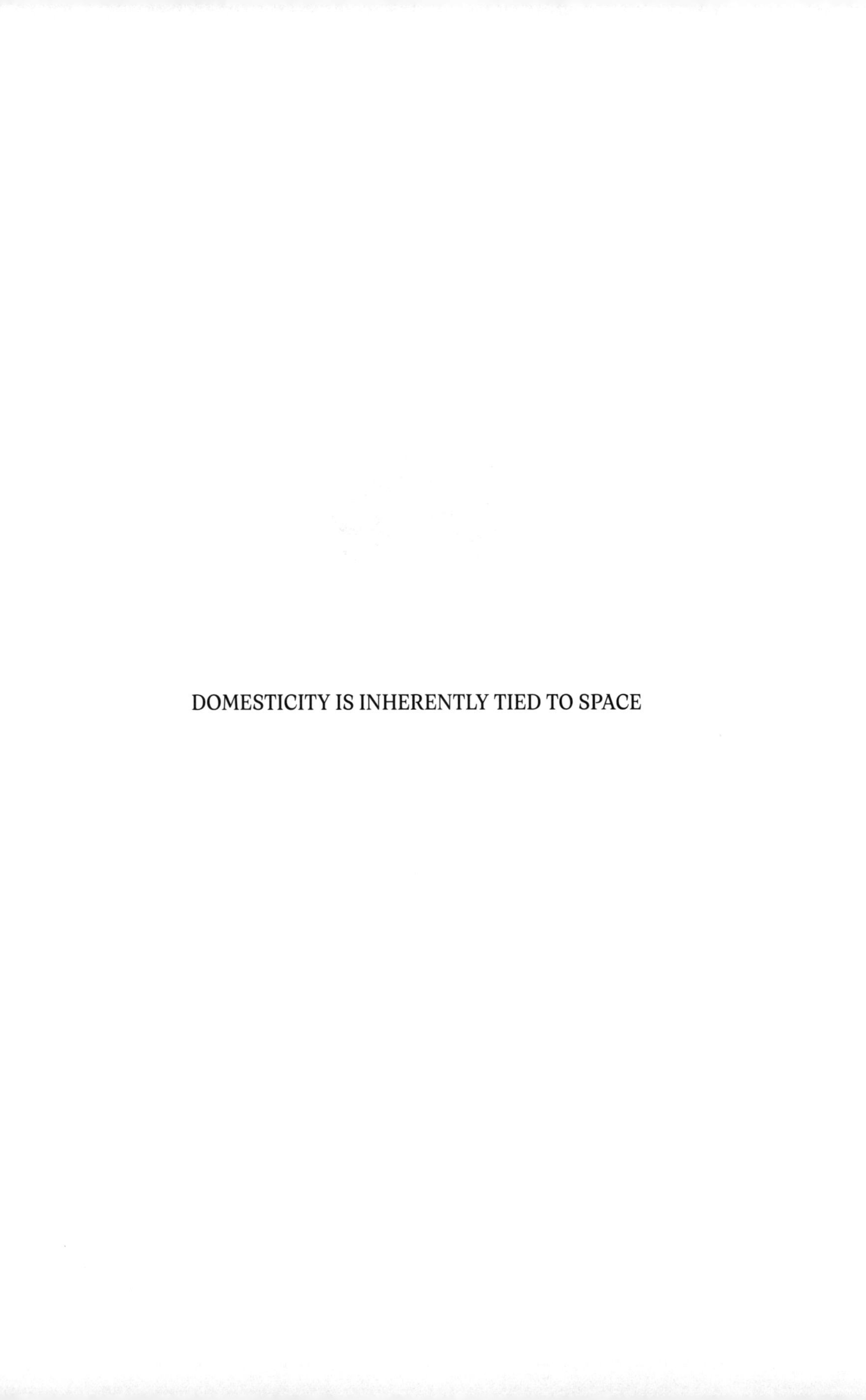

DOMESTICITY IS INHERENTLY TIED TO SPACE

3+ participants

No materials needed

INSTRUCTIONS *(version 1)*

* Hold hands to form a closed human chain.
* Maintaining this formation, and without talking, we invite you to explore the space of the home as long as needed.

How to explore a space differently by compromising with the other.

Coordination and collaboration must be practiced.

Starting with 6+ participants

No materials needed

INSTRUCTIONS *(version 2)*

⁕ Hold hands to form an open human chain.
⁕ Starting from an open door inside your home, we invite you to extend the human chain one by one: How far can we reach? Where would you go? What could we do?

TIPS: If going outdoors, you can involve people on the street to get where you want to be.

How do we embody the privilege to be in a certain place?
Where does that privilege come from and how do we compromise with it?

In a hyper individualistic society, the collective body is always compromising the freedom of the individual.
This exercise aims to practice collective awareness, collaborative thinking and problem-solving.

Individual

Paper and drawing tools or alternatively magazines, scissors, glue (for collage), or just a journal for keywords

INSTRUCTIONS

* Take a moment to observe your current living space. Draw a simple representation of your home. Focus on the layout, key furniture, and any elements that define your space (like windows, doors, or favorite items). If drawing isn't comfortable, you can use keywords or phrases that describe your home. You can also create a small collage using cut-out images that resonate with your current living situation.
* After completing your drawing or collage, take a few minutes to reflect on how you feel about your current space. Consider the following prompts: What do you love about it? What would you like to change or improve?
* Draw or create a collage of your dream space.
Think about elements like: the atmosphere, colors and materials, and spaces.

This exercise is an invitation to a first hands on intervention in our domestic environment, encouraging you to visualize your surroundings and embrace imagination, but also take over the responsibility of what it means to design a home. By contrasting the current home with an imaginative space, one can gain clarity on what truly matters to their living environment, while challenging the traditional means of interior design and architecture, disciplines which can be perceived far from who really, in the end, inhabits a space.

How many ways and designs can we imagine for our homes?

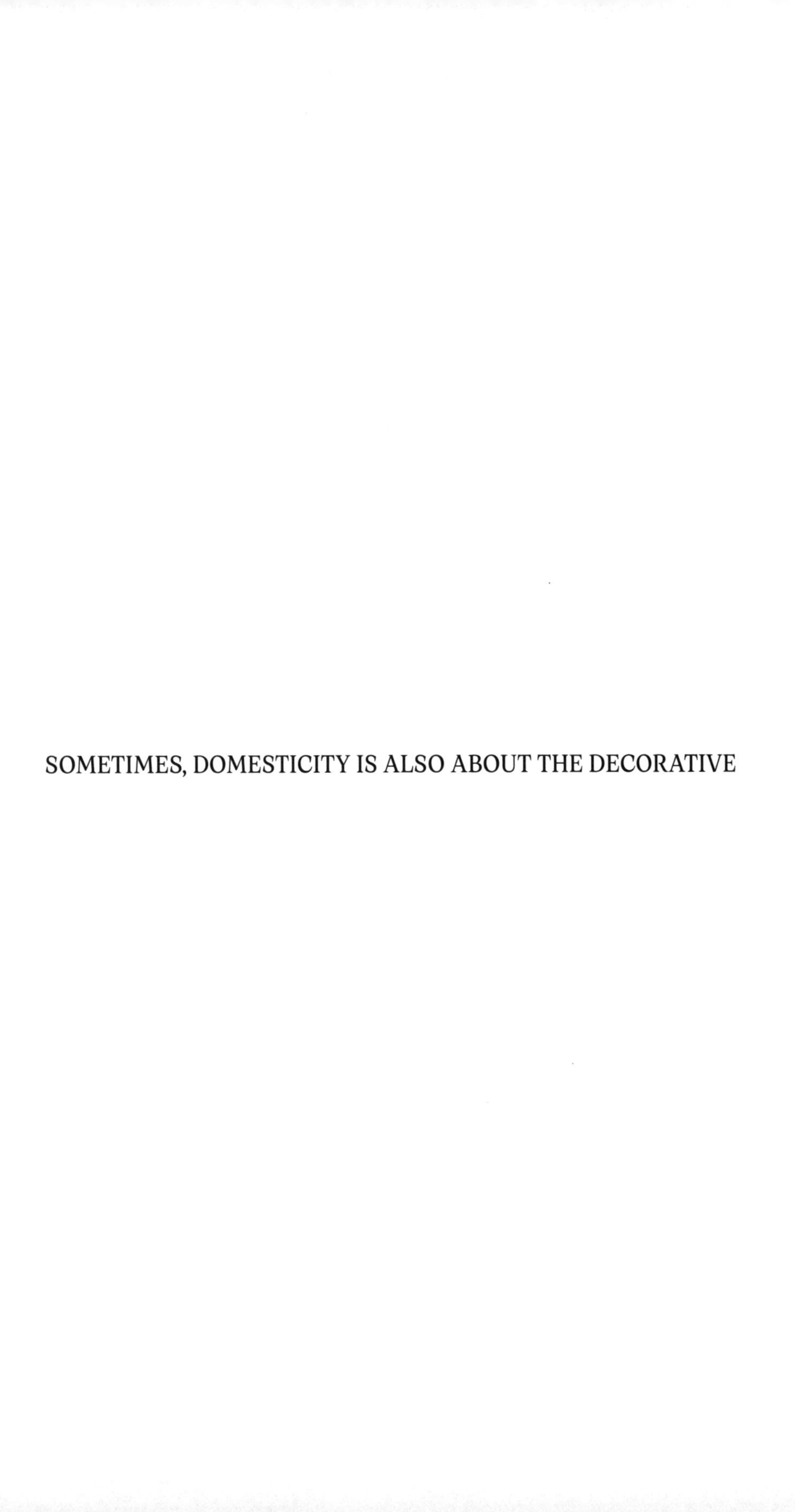

SOMETIMES, DOMESTICITY IS ALSO ABOUT THE DECORATIVE

What do you consider decorative in your living space?

Is it something additional, extra, or is it essential to call a space "home"?

What does decoration mean to you?

6 + Participants

No materials needed

INSTRUCTIONS

(version 1)
bodies as decoration

✳ You are inside a space considered a home. Using your bodies, we invite each of you to select a repetitive movement or a brief sequence of movements that symbolize an aspect of the decorative dimension within your home. This could mimic a decorative item, an interior feature, or convey a particular emotion. In either case, the movements should provide additional emotional insight into your chosen object or feeling.

Exercise developments: One person at a time will take on the role of the guest.
The others, silently, will disperse throughout the space of the home and adopt a starting posture to hold. As the guest passes by each participant, they can initiate their movement. Allow the guest to explore and engage with each movement.

INSTRUCTIONS

(version 2)
voices as decoration

⁕ Similar to the previous exercise, but using sounds. Participants can produce sounds using their voice, hands, or a tool (including a musical instrument).
⁕ Additionally, an appointed participant may act as a director to guide the ensemble.

This exercise fosters a horizontal approach to research, utilizing the body or voice as mediums for conveying concepts or emotions. It encourages an alternative exploration of the intimate connections shaping our own and others' living spaces.

What constitutes a home?

This series of exercises invites you to engage deeply with the objects in your home, prompting reflection on the choices we make and how these choices shape our living spaces.

Individual, you may also choose to engage with others simultaneously

No materials needed

INSTRUCTIONS *(version 1)*

⁕ We invite you to select an object from your home and spend at least one hour with it. Consider taking the object for a walk or enjoying a coffee together.
Alternatively, simply move it outside its usual location and experiment with different actions.

INSTRUCTIONS *(version 2)*

⁕ We invite you to choose an object from your home and spend at least one hour with it. During this time, imagine the object as an active agent with its own thoughts and feelings. Write from the object's perspective, giving it a voice.

Consider the following prompts to guide your writing: What stories does the object have to tell? How does it feel about its place in your home? What experiences has it witnessed in its lifetime? How does it perceive the humans who interact with it?

INSTRUCTIONS *(version 3)*

⁕ Select an object from your home and dedicate a chosen amount of time to performing a repetitive action with it. This could be anything from stacking, rearranging, or even cleaning the object.

As you engage in this action, pay attention to the rhythm it creates and the feelings that arise. *Reflect on the following:* How does the repetition affect your perception of the object? Does the action transform the object's significance or your relationship with it? What thoughts or emotions surface as you repeat the action?

What meanings do we infuse into our objects? How confined are we by our preconceptions of what makes an object decorative and what defines a home?

This exercise encourages you to explore new perspectives and reflect on the relationship between objects and their surroundings.

How do we perceive our homes?
Do we move differently in a space we own compared to one that we don't (we may rent or sublet)? This iteration explores the relationships between spaces and ownership, including the objects and infrastructure within them. How does this dynamic influence our daily lives in a domestic setting? This ties into the concept of care – do people tend to care less for things they don't own?

Individual

No materials needed

INSTRUCTIONS

✳ The exercise could be done by writing or by performing. It can include all categories or focus on one only. It can also be performed with own's body: for example, you are free to choose a thing* and perform different movements, feelings, or sounds that establish your relationship with it.

A list of things:*
I own
I do not own
I am responsible for
I am not responsible for

*In regards of these things**
I feel detached from
I feel connected to
I feel responsible for
I do not feel responsible for

How do I perceive my body in relation to these things:*
Close/Distant
Safe/unsafe
Etc.

What do I do for/with these things:*
I perform movements and actions
I perform feelings and care
I perform:

How much time (daily or weekly) I spend with/for these things:*
None
Minutes
Hours
Days
Etc.

**with the world things we invite you to resonate with the elements of your home, the material (from the architecture, the objects, etc) and the immaterial (the digital or legal infrastructures, for example).*

BUT DON'T FORGET ABOUT HOSPITALITY!

6 + Participants

Inside an empty space

INSTRUCTIONS

(version 1)

inviting a passer-by
to have coffee in your kitchen

⁕ Without planning ahead, compose a line. The first one in line will perform the stepl of the choreography with a movement or a series of movements (the number of steps vary depending on the number of participants).
⁕ The second person will follow once the first has completed their movements/series of movements.
⁕ One person of the group must then perform as the passer-by and experience the gesture of hospitality.

ATT: The same exercise can be done without agreeing upon the suggested invitation.
The concept of hospitality can be interpreted freely by the group and embody as a whole.

Practicing hospitality *through small gestures*

as a collective body who then will shape the space where hospitality actually happens.
The space is shaped by a choreography of care and not the other way around.

INSTRUCTIONS *(version 2)*

*A group of people invite a passer-by to have coffee in their kitchen (a real coffee, then).

P r a c t i c i n g hospitality.

Afterwords

A Room of Our Own:
Cecilia Casabona in conversation with Ilaria and Georgina

Principles of inclusivity, openness, and cooperation characterized the whole making of this publication. Certainly, by carrying out this project, our perspective on domesticity and the complexities there embedded, has evolved. The ongoing research has been a source of enrichment, a learning progress, a moment to consolidate past encounters and to make new ones. Through an intersectional feminist lens, we pursue situated knowledge marked by perspectives that are partial rather than universal, and that are embodied rather than neutral. In developing this publication, we were inspired by Alison Place's reflections in *Feminist Designer: On the Personal and the Political in Design.* She challenges the idea that designers should separate their professional and personal selves, emphasizing instead that our perspectives and lived experiences inevitably shape our work. Rather than seeing this as a limitation, acknowledging our positionality allows us to uncover hidden power structures within the design process. Likewise, recognizing our own biases and internalized assumptions becomes a crucial step toward a more reflective and responsible practice.

The conclusions of this publication take the form of a dialogue with Cecilia Casabona, reflecting on our positions as individuals and designers. Maintaining a dialogical mindset has been fundamental throughout this research, and choosing to conclude the publication in the same spirit prompted us to consider the practical applications of this research journey. This discussion serves as a moment of appreciation for the topic itself; a conversation between three people about home, about the domestic and the intimate. A reflection on how these spaces connect us to our personal center and the ways in which we find our way back to it.

CECILIA Within the current crisis surrounding the concept of "home", you aim to rethink and reimagine domestic spaces through your research and practice. How does this rethinking work and how do you position yourselves as architects, as feminists, as human beings as well?

GEORGINA One of the reasons Ilaria and I started this project is exactly the context you describe. Coming to The Netherlands as expats we encountered difficulties. It was hard for us to, firstly, find a house and, most importantly, to find a house that we will feel as home. When, in the second year of the Master in Interior Architecture, we had to choose a research topic that would develop into a graduation project, I immediately felt drawn to working on something related to domesticity. At that point, I realized that as an architect, I had never experienced designing proposals related to house interiors with a critical perspective. Starting with the graduation project, I noticed that a critical approach to the topic is indeed very relevant. And after several discussions till today, three years later, I think it still is. That is why we initiated and we continue this research, positioning ourselves as practitioners on this side of contemporary design practice; the side that takes a critical perspective, questioning and reflecting on the past, present, and future of the spatial realm. I feel proud that as an architect and designer I always try, including this publication, to find alternative ways of designing a home and to explain why not every design of a house is the design of a home. Researching domesticity, especially through an intersectional feminist lens, has given purpose to my design career and practice. While studying architecture and later working in architectural studios, I always felt that something was missing. Yes, we were designing interiors, but why? In most cases, I couldn't see a true identity in the spaces we created. It was also difficult for me to understand why we didn't engage with clients - the future inhabitants of these spaces - on a more personal level. Why weren't we taking the time to understand their experiences, their sense of familiarity, and their personal attachments? Building an intimate dialogue with them could lead to spatial designs that genuinely reflect and nurture intimacy. Of course, another important aspect of approaching this research was my own unique and intimate story. My personal connection to the topic of domesticity, my experiences, my past, and how these sometimes shape the present.

ILARIA I also share Gerogina's experience a bit. I feel like we have been "called" to join this discourse. My personal journey is quite particular. Coming from interior design studies, I always believed I was already part of the conversation on domesticity. However, I recently realized that I had never approached it with a critical lens. More importantly, I understood that practicing interior design alone does not necessarily engage with the deeper concepts behind domesticity. The way I was educated in the spatial field was based on a strict contrast between interior and exterior worlds. No one really taught me how to put these two spheres in dialogue. I had the

first relevant conversation about that with Georgina just a couple of years ago. We both position ourselves in this conversation because, as mentioned, we feel "called" and that is because our personal experiences regarding this topic are quite strong. Of course, we engage in this from a place of privilege, as we have the freedom to choose our starting point in the conversation. However, we want to emphasize - especially in this publication - how much personal experience matters when designing domestic spaces. I have worked in architectural offices where the primary goal of designing domestic spaces was to generate capital - which, in a way, is understandable. I've lost count of how many times I've seen designs that minimize square meters just to maximize the number of apartment units.
I think the moment that pushed me toward this research came a couple of years ago when I found myself split between two drastically different realities: working in an interior design office, designing homes for the wealthy, while simultaneously researching the intimate living spaces of asylum seekers' centers. I asked myself: *Who am I?* I started to think more critically about my role within the topic of domesticity and the design of home.

Georgina and I are trying to show that there is much more behind a simple floor plan or section. Domestic spaces are shaped by complex relationships; it is not only about how good an architect can be in making an interesting and functional layout, or choosing the right furniture and lighting. It is about creating spaces where the political dimensions of home can be expressed and experienced. After all, truly feeling at home in a space requires acknowledging the personal and social layers that define domesticity.

GEORGINA Of course we can do it in practice and we can design a house in practice, but for us it is very important to understand how and why we do that. We live in a capitalist era, we consume everything. For us, it is essential to know what the past of everyone is, their origin, tradition or cultural background and how this is reflected inside the home environment. For example, why do so many homes in the Western world have white walls, white kitchens, gray floors, and gray bathrooms? What does that say about the people who inhabit these spaces? When I moved to the Netherlands, I only brought my clothes with me, but my world is so much more than that. Architects should strive to connect with the real needs of users, considering the deeper layers of identity and experience when designing a home.

ILARIA Yes, and for that very reason, through our research and this publication, we aim to explore and introduce tools to facilitate both architects and users to achieve this. The second part of this book presents a series of exercises designed to encourage readers - whether designers, users, architects, or individuals - to perceive their domestic environments differently. These exercises invite reflection on the actions, rituals, habits, and roles that shape daily life at home. While this is just a first step for us, it is essential to create a space within this research where its findings can be

tested. This section serves as a dynamic invitation to experiment with new ways of understanding and engaging with domesticity.

CECILIA You look at domesticity through a multidisciplinary approach, why did you choose to opt for this open approach? What then is domesticity for you? What is the feminist lens that you use in connection to what you just said? What are the tools that can make this approach more open, can you make some examples?

ILARIA We might not always realize it, but architecture itself is already a multidisciplinary discipline since it intersects at the same time with so many political and social aspects of life. However, the design of spaces does not always reflect this complexity. Too often, it remains tied to the figure - or "role" - of the architect, a legacy of modernism that we are committed to challenging. We were experiencing the shortcomings of addressing the topic of domesticity solely through a spatial lens and, therefore, quite directly engaged with multiple perspectives. It's quite funny; while we often emphasize that this publication includes multiple voices - which is true - many of them still come from within the architectural and design sphere. However, what matters the most to us, is that these contributions do not strictly adhere to conventional architectural ways of understanding space but they bring in other possibilities. You asked for examples, and the best ones come from sharing our collective experiences. In conversations with practitioners, through contributions and in our workshops, this idea emerged repeatedly. The feminist perspective we engage with is fundamentally about redistributing the knowledge to shape domestic space - ensuring that everyone has the agency to claim and define their own living environment.

GEORGINA An intersectional feminist approach to the domestic environment comes naturally to us. The multilayered nature of domesticity demands such an approach. After all, how can we truly design familiar and inclusive environments if we do not consider diversity in terms of gender, age, race, class, ability, and cultural or geographical background? Because every familiarity is different, we believe that approaching the domestic environment necessitates an intersectional feminist framework. We were overwhelmed by 20th-century modernist architecture, which often became an elitist framework. Designing a house according to that model is almost the opposite of what a domestic environment should be. An intersectional feminist approach reminds us that modernism is not the only possible design perspective; something we also learned during our studies. Instead, domesticity is complex and multidimensional, requiring tools and methods that reflect this understanding.

CECILIA I have a bit of a provocative question: Isn't your approach somewhat elitist – at least for now? It's quite unique and requires a lot of care, which I know you have, but more importantly, it demands time and space - both of which are scarce in today's crisis. How do

you ensure that your methodology and approach are truly accessible to everyone? How do you create the time and space needed for others to engage with it?

ILARIA Rather than offering fixed solutions, we see this work as a starting point for ongoing dialogue and experimentation, creating frameworks that others can appropriate and reshape according to their needs and realities. By choosing to detach this publication from the academic framework, we feel we are taking small but meaningful steps to facilitate conversations that need to happen. I can say that at every stage of this publication's development, we have actively worked to deconstruct our own assumptions and the methods we were used to.

GEORGINA We also use examples to make our thoughts and practice more accessible and understandable. As Ilaria said, this publication is not an academic one; we want it to be readable and useful for anyone, even those without a background in spatial design or feminist theory. While we gained this knowledge through our education, we do not expect others to have it. That is why this research and publication are grounded in personal and lived experiences. Our goal is for this book to be multifaceted and multilayered, making it more accessible to a wider audience.

ILARIA The idea behind this publication is that by sharing experiences, we invite others to do the same and start their own conversations. Even for us, what made us start this research came from sharing personal experiences with one another. We present stories that people can relate to - or, in some cases, contrast with - encouraging reflection on domesticity in its many forms. For a long time, we referred to these stories as "case studies" but, as Georgina pointed out, they are examples. This is not a book to be read all at once from beginning to end. Rather, it's a book you can navigate, free to find your way in the story that is closest to your personal experiences regarding domestic life, or perhaps one that is the opposite of it.

CECILIA Your approach is very participatory. I think of your last intervention during Milan Design Week, "home-work." [137] Can you tell us more about the way you design a new workshop? Why is the participatory dimension so important for you and what does it add to your research and practice?

GEORGINA We always consider the context in which we conduct our workshops. The approach we take in

137
We were invited to host a workshop at DOPO? Space during Milan Design Week 2024, where the venue was transformed into a co-living space - offering artists and designers a rare opportunity for accessible accommodation in exchange for exhibition space. We developed "Home-Work", a role-play workshop exploring what it means to share a temporary home with strangers while exhibiting at a major design event. The workshop highlighted the dual nature of this experience - where living and working overlap, raising questions about when domestic space fosters conviviality and when it risks becoming extractive. Through role-playing, participants reflected on these dynamics, shared personal experiences, and collaboratively created live images - reimagining the space beyond its function as an exhibition and temporary accommodation.

Asylum Seekers Centers, for example, is naturally different from the one we use in educational or cultural contexts. While many of our workshops focus on domesticity, we are equally interested in the background of each participant. This forms the foundation of our method. From there, we develop questions and steps, always remaining open to hearing the voices in the room. In many cases, the workshops are shaped by the participants themselves. We design a workshop, but its execution can vary significantly depending on who takes part.

ILARIA First of all, I think I can say we really love workshops. There is a learning process for everybody. We give the possibility to everyone to speak equally and we explore different tools for this to happen - drawing, writing, embroidery, talking. Not everyone is comfortable speaking, and not everyone enjoys drawing, so we remain flexible, allowing participants to choose what feels most natural to them. For us, it's fascinating to see how domesticity can be explored across different contexts. That's also what this book does - it addresses the topic from multiple perspectives and within different situations.

GEORGINA We really love doing workshops, and this topic indeed fits within the workshop format. As mentioned before, we use examples to explore it, and through workshops, we can invite everyone to participate, bringing in diverse voices and perspectives.

ILARIA Maybe something to mention is that our workshops are always free of charge. In the way we operate, we try to stick to certain principles, to make this topic accessible from this perspective as well. There are so many sacrifices that we are making to achieve what we want to do. I think it is important to be honest with what our process is. At the same time, I also recognize that the concept of a workshop itself can feel somewhat elitist - not everyone is familiar with it. I've encountered many situations where people didn't really know what a workshop was. That's why we also think about how to shift the focus away from just the final results and instead create a space for meaningful conversations. Our workshops are never meant to create a physically completed outcome, quite the opposite; the focus is on the process and on what can emerge from that.

CECILIA Have you ever thought about how this can work in an architectural firm?

GEORGINA We want to put these ideas into practice. A big challenge for me would be designing my own house - if I ever had the opportunity to do so from the ground up. My personal belief, which Ilaria also shares, is that education plays a crucial role in shaping our design approach. Currently, I am pursuing a PhD focused on the domestic environment through an educational lens. If we train ourselves from the early stages of our careers to approach the design of homes, or spaces in general, through an inclusive and feminist framework, then integrating these principles into architectural practice will come more naturally when working in a studio. If we are already trained to think

not only about functionality (which is, of course, very important) but also within this framework, then when we collaborate with other people and clients, keeping these principles in mind may make it easier to arrive at a result that truly reflects the personality of those who inhabit the space. It's also crucial to follow this approach during the design process itself. If the design process within a team or studio is rooted in intersectional feminism and mutual respect, the outcome will likely reflect these values. And perhaps, we can achieve something even better.

CECILIA What led you to take on the role of curators for this publication rather than positioning yourselves as designers or architects? Why did you make this choice? How do you see the role of the architect today? What was it like to step away from your background and take on a different role? Has this experience given you a new or deeper understanding of domesticity, and if so, how would you define it now?

ILARIA The idea of making this publication came a couple of years ago, but we didn't do it straight away. We explored different things, met different people, and got to know about different practices. One day we looked each other in the eyes and wondered which would be the best way to express everything we encountered, everything we had to say, and everything the people we met had to say as well. We see ourselves as facilitators, so then the idea of curating and editing these contributions and putting them all together in a publication was quite a spontaneous act. It is very nice that everyone who is part of this publication is someone we came across with and whose experience we envisioned to be relevant for our research. Once more the personal experiences came at hand. By taking this editor role we also want to understand which are the things that we still have to discover, because we are really learning. Giving voices to the practitioners we met along our research and combining them with our practices, means for us to present a vision from the current generation of designers that surrounds us. I was also having a conversation with a friend yesterday about how nowadays we encounter books that, just like this one, are a collective effort. There is a movement happening to share ideas, goals, difficulties; a movement to come together; a movement of voices. This really gives me hope.

GEORGINA I feel that this book is not the end of the journey but rather the beginning of something for us. This is not a project that we simply complete and close; it is part of a lifelong research, and this is just a moment of reflection. And, by sharing this journey with others, we've learned so much. I believe many things will follow after this book. Who knows, maybe in five or ten years, we will be able to define the approach we follow to create a more inclusive domestic environment. Maybe we'll discover the *methodology*, or maybe we won't. But I think we'll continue exploring this topic for as long as we need to. Especially in these times of crisis, having a house that feels like a home - a place of intimacy - must be prioritized. We've achieved so much, yet this issue is still there.

ILARIA We dream of one day having our academy, where we can establish and test these new methodologies we are exploring regarding the domestic environment. It's also important to mention that the research presented in this publication brings together people at different stages of their practice, with the aim of connecting a younger, emerging set of voices with those who are already putting these ideas into action.

Acknowledgments

ACKNOWLEDGMENTS

We wish to express our gratitude to everyone who supported us throughout the process of this publication. Special thanks go to the Graham Foundation for Advanced Studies in the Fine Arts and to Stimuleringsfonds for their generous support, without which this book would not be in your hands.

A sincere thank you to the contributors of this publication for trusting us on this adventurous journey, for enriching our perspectives, and for believing in us and in the urgency of the conversations held within (and beyond) these pages. Your voices remind us why these dialogues matter and deserve to be shared. Thank you to Alice, Cecilia, Davide, Diederik, Feven, Ines, Kevin, Laura, Lara, Michele, Noemi, Panos, Platon, Ramón, Rising, Setareh, Sophie, Sophia, Susanna, Vida, and Valentina.

We would like to acknowledge Anna and Noemi for their careful and curious approach to editing the book's text, and Elisa for her magical eye and touch in the graphic design. A huge thank you to Freek for believing in this project from the very beginning and for guiding us with care and insight as our publisher. Finally, our deepest gratitude goes to our families and friends for their confidence, support, and trust.

Last but not least, a warm thank you to one another – to us, Ilaria and Georgina – for choosing to begin this journey together, and for all the inspired, generous moments we have shared along the way over these past years.

introduction

Ahmed, Sara. "Home and Away: Narratives of Migration and Estrangement." *International Journal of Cultural Studies 2,* no. 3 (December 1, 1999): 329–47.

Awan, Nishat, Tatjana Schneider, and Jeremy Till. *Spatial Agency: Other Ways of Doing Architecture.* Routledge, 2013.

Baydar, Gülsüm, and Hilde Heynen. *Negotiating Domesticity: Spatial Productions of Gender in Modern Architecture.* Routledge, 2005.

Beeckmans, Luce, Alessandra Gola, Ashika Singh, and Hilde Heynen, eds. *Making Home(s) in Displacement: Critical Reflections on a Spatial Practice.* Leuven University Press, 2022.

Beeckmans, Luce, Ashika Singh, and Alessandra Gola. "Rethinking the Intersection of Home and Displacement from a Spatial Perspective." In *Making Home(s) in Displacement,* edited by Luce Beeckmans, Ashika Singh, Alessandra Gola, and Hilde Heynen, 11–42. Critical Reflections on a Spatial Practice. Leuven University Press, 2022.

Costanza-Chock, Sasha. *Design Justice: Community-Led Practices to Build the Worlds We Need.* MIT Press, 2020.

Harriss, Harriet, and Emily Eliza Scott. "What Forms Might Feminist Pedagogy Take in Architecture and Who Are Its Potential Protagonists (Imaginary or Real)?" *Making Trouble to Stay With: Architecture and Feminist Pedagogies,* 2017.

Hayden, Dolores. *The Grand Domestic Revolution: A History of Feminist Designs for American Homes, Neighborhoods and Cities.* MIT Press, 2000.

Kern, Leslie. *Feminist City: Claiming Space in a Man-Made World.* Verso Books, 2020.

Lange, Torsten, Emely E. Scott, Lila Athanasiadou, Harriet Harriss, Andrea J. Merrett, Iradj Moeini, Jane Rendell, and Rachel Sara. "Making Trouble to Stay With: Architecture and Feminist Pedagogies." *Field 7,* no. 1 (November 2017): 89–99.

Le Corbusier. *The Modulor.* Faber & Faber, 1961.

Mareis, Claudia, and Nina Paim, eds. *Design Struggles: Intersecting Histories, Pedagogies, and Perspectives.* Valiz, 2021.

Martinis, Roe Alex. *To Become Two - Propositions for Feminist Collective Practice.* Archive Books, 2018.

Massey, Doreen. *Space, Place and Gender.* Polity Press, 2007.

Pitard, Jayne. "View of A Journey to the Centre of Self: Positioning the Researcher in Autoethnography | Forum Qualitative Sozialforschung / Forum: Qualitative Social Research." *Forum Qualitative Sozialforschung / Forum: Qualitative Social Research 18,* no. 3 (September 2017).

Place, Alison. *Feminist Designer: On the Personal and the Political in Design.* MIT Press, 2023.

Rice, Charles. *The Emergence of the Interior: Architecture, Modernity, Domesticity.* Routledge, 2007.

Rybczynski, Witold. *Home: A Short History of an Idea.* Penguin Books, 1987.

Sandercock, Leonie, and Ann Forsyth. "A Gender Agenda: New Directions for Planning Theory." *Journal of The American Planning Association* (March 31, 1992): 49–59.

Sanderson, Laura, and Sally Stone, eds. *Emerging Practices in Architectural Pedagogy: Accommodating an Uncertain Future.* Routledge, 2021.

Tayob, Huda, and Suzanne Hall. *Race, Space and Architecture: Towards and Open-Access Curriculum.* London, UK: London School of Economics and Political Science, Department of Sociology, 2019.

Verschaffel, Bart. "The Meanings of Domesticity." *The Journal of Architecture 7,* no. 3 (January 1, 2002): 287-96.

Winton, Alexa. "Inhabited Space: Critical Theories and the Domestic Interior." In *The Handbook of Interior Architecture and Design,* 40-49, 2013.

from the balcony

Beauvoir, Simone de. *The Second Sex.* Vintage Classics, 1956.

Brookfield, Harold. I*nterdependent Development.* Methuen, 1975.

Caleo, Ilenia. "Performing (Art) Institutions. Contro l'autonomia dell'estetico." *Connessioni Remote,* II, 2, 2021: 136-145.

Delz, Sascha. "Spatial Dialogic." In *Lessons of Informality: Architecture and Urban Planning for Emerging Territories. Concepts from Ethiopia,* edited by Felix Heisel and Bisrat Kifle Woldeyessus, 190-200. Birkhäuser, 2016.

Disalvo, Carl. *Adversarial Design.* MIT Press, 2012.

Hebel, Dirk, and Elias Yitbarek. "Addis Ababa - Extracting Character From Voids." In *Building Ethiopia,* edited by Zegeye Cherenet and Helawi Sewnet. EiABC, 2012.

Heisel, Felix. "Housing Typologies - A Case Study in Addis Ababa." In *Building Ethiopia,* edited by Zegeye Cherenet and Helawi Sewnet, 263-69. EiABC, 2012.

Le Corbusier. *The Modulor.* Faber & Faber, 1961.

Le Corbusier. *Towards a New Architecture.* Dover Publications, 2021.

Makimoto, Tsugio, and David Manners. *Digital Nomad.* Wiley, 1997.

Maldonado, Tomás. *La speranza progettuale. Ambiente e società.* Feltrinelli, 2022.

Mann, Thomas. *Death in Venice.* Knopf, 1965.

Pieterse, Edgar. "Cityness and African Urban Development." *Urban Forum 21,* no. 3 (1 August 2010): 205-19.

———. "Grasping the Unknowable: Coming to Grips with African Urbanisms." *Social Dynamics 37,* no. 1 (March 2011): 5-23.

Salerno, Giacomo-Maria, and Antonio Paolo Russo. "Venice as a Short-Term City. Between Global Trends and Local Lock-Ins." *Journal of Sustainable Tourism XXX,* no. 5 (4 May 2022): 1040-59.

Settis, Salvatore. *If Venice Dies.* New Vessel Press, 2016. https://newvesselpress.com/books/if-venice-dies/.

Vanhee, Sarah. "The Fantastic Institutions." *Nu in de Kunsten,* August 20, 2022. https://www.kunsten.be/nu-in-de-kunsten/the-fantastic-institutions/

under the carpet

Ahmed, Sara. *Queer Phenomenology: Orientations, Objects, Others.* Duke University Press, 2006.

Baudrillard, Jean. *The System of Objects.* Verso Books, 2020.

Boyarsky, Nicholas. "House X." In *Activism at Home: Architects Dwelling between Politics, Aesthetics and Resistance,* edited by Isabelle Doucet and Janina Gosseye, 159–70. Jovis, 2021.

Briganti, Chiara, and Kathy Mezei. *The Domestic Space Reader.* University of Toronto Press, 2012.

Chee, Lilian. "Domesticity, Gender, and Architecture." In *The Routledge Companion to Contemporary Architectural History.* Routledge, 2023.

Chu, Yiu-Wai, ed. *Hong Kong Culture and Society in the New Millennium. Vol. 4. The Humanities in Asia.* Singapore: Springer, 2017.

Colomina, Beatriz, and Jennifer Bloomer. *Sexuality & Space.* Princeton Architectural Press, 1992.

Crenshaw, Kimberle. "Mapping the Margins: Intersectionality, Identity Politics, and Violence against Women of Color." *Stanford Law Review 43,* no. 6 (1991): 1241–99.

Eisen, Markus. *Vom Ledigenheim zum Boardinghouse: Bautypologie und Gesellschaftstheorie bis zum Ende der Weimarer Republik.* Gebr. Mann Verlag, 2012.

Giolli Menni, Rosa. "La Casa Di Una Donna Sola." *Eva 1,* no. 8 (April 1933).

Haraway, Donna. "Situated Knowledges: The Science Question in Feminism and the Privilege of Partial Perspective." *Feminist Studies 14,* no. 3 (1988): 575–99.

Harriss, Harriet, and Naomi House. "Interiority Complex." In *A Gendered Profession.* RIBA Publishing, 2019.

Heynen, Hilde, and Gülsüm Baydar, eds. *Negotiating Domesticity: Spatial Productions of Gender in Modern Architecture.* Routledge, 2005.

hooks, bell. "Choosing the Margin as a Space of Radical Openness." *Framework: The Journal of Cinema and Media,* no. 36 (1989): 15–23.

'In Memoriam. Luigi Buffoli'. Stabilimento Tipografico dell'Unione Cooperativa - Milano, 1911.

Lopez, Guillermo, and Anna Puigjaner. "Everyday Life in the Diffuse House." In *Everyday Matters: Contemporary Approaches to Architecture,* edited by Vanessa Grossman and Ciro Miguel. Ruby Press, 2021.

Perec, Georges. *Species of Spaces and Other Pieces.* Penguin Books, 1997.

Place, Alison. *Feminist Designer: On the Personal and the Political in Design.* MIT Press, 2023.

Pugni, Gianfranco. *C'era Una Volta l'albergo. La Vicenda Dell'Albergo Popolare Di Milano.* CRAL Ospedale S. Paolo, 2001.

Sanderson, Laura, and Sally Stone, eds. *Emerging Practices in Architectural Pedagogy: Accommodating an Uncertain Future.* Routledge, 2021.

Schmidt, Ariadne, Isabelle Devos, and Bruno Blondé. "Single and the City: Men and Women Alone in North-Western European Towns since the Late Middle Ages." In *Single Life and the City 1200–1900,* edited by Julie De Groot, Isabelle Devos, and Ariadne Schmidt, 1–24. Palgrave Macmillan UK, 2015.

Scola, Ettore. *Una Giornata Particolare* (1977).

Weisman, Leslie Kanes. "Re-Designing Architectural Education: New Models for a New Century." In *Design and Feminism: Re-Visioning Spaces, Places, and Everyday Things,* edited by Joan Rothschild and Alethea Cheng. Rutgers University Press, 1999, 159–173.

Young, Iris Marion. "House and Home: Feminist Variations on a Theme." In *Motherhood and Space: Configurations of the Maternal through Politics, Home, and the Body,* edited by Sarah Hardy and Caroline Wiedmer, 115–47. Palgrave Macmillan, 2005.

through the door

Ahmed, Sara. *Queer Phenomenology: Orientations, Objects, Others.* Duke University Press, 2006.

Ahmed, Sara. *Strange Encounters: Embodied Others in Post-Coloniality.* Routledge, 2000.

Barad, Karen. "After the End of the World: Matters of Hospitality." In *Rehearsing Hospitalities: Companion 3,* edited by Yvonne Billimore and Jussi Koitela. Archive Books, 2021.

Barrett, Michèle, and Mary McIntosh. *The Anti-Social Family.* Verso Books, 2015.

Beeckmans, Luce, Ashika Singh, and Alessandra Gola. "Rethinking the Intersection of Home and Displacement from a Spatial Perspective." In *Making Home(s) in Displacement,* edited by Luce Beeckmans, Ashika Singh, Alessandra Gola, and Hilde Heynen, 11–42. Leuven University Press, 2022.

Braidotti, Rosi. *The Posthuman.* Polity, 2013.

Brun, Cathrine, and Anita Fábos. "Making Homes in Limbo? A Conceptual Framework." *Refuge 31,* no. 2 (April 2015): 5–17.

Dauphinee, Elizabeth. "The Ethics of Autoethnography." *Review of International Studies 36,* no. 3 (2010): 799–818.

De Craen, Irene, and Merve Bedir. "On Solidarity, Community and Landscape." *Errant Journal,* no. 4 (2022): 89–100.

Despret, Vinciane. *Living as a Bird.* Polity, 2021.

Derrida, Jacques. *Of Hospitality.* Stanford University Press, 2000.

Dreyer, Maretha. "Years in the Waiting Room: A Feminist Ethnography of the Invisible Institutional Living Spaces of Forced Displacement." In *Making Home(s) in Displacement,* edited by Luce Beeckmans, Alessandra Gola, Ashika Singh, and Hilde Heynen, 197–218. Leuven University Press, 2022. https://doi.org/10.2307/j.ctv25wxbvf.12.

Dufourmantelle, Anne, and Catherine Malabou. *Power of Gentleness: Meditations on the Risk of Living.* Translated by Katherine Payne and Vincent Sall. Fordham University Press, 2018.

Etherington, Kim. *Becoming a Reflexive Researcher: Using Our Selves in Research.* Jessica Kingsley Publishers, 2004.

Federici, Silvia. *Re-Enchanting the World: Feminism and the Politics of the Commons.* PM Press, 2018.

Flesler, Griselda, Anja Neidhardt, and Maya Ober. "NOT A TOOLKIT. A Conversation on the Discomfort of Feminist Design Pedagogy." In *Design Struggles. Intersecting Histories, Pedagogies, and Perspectives,* edited by Claudia Mareis and Nina Paim, 205–25. Valiz, with Swiss Design Network SDN.

Hamington, Maurice. "Toward a Theory of Feminist Hospitality." *Feminist Formations 22,* no. 1 (2010): 21–38.

Haraway, Donna J. "Making Kin in the Chthulucene: Reproducing Multispecies Justice." In *Making Kin Not Population*, edited by Adele Clarke and Donna J. Haraway, 67–100. Prickly Paradigm Press, 2018.

Heeswijk, Jeanne van. "Preparing for the Not-Yet." In *Slow Reader: A Resource for Design Thinking and Practice,* edited by Ana Paula Pais and Carolyn F. Strauss. Valiz, 2016.

Jeanniard du Dot, Maëlle, and Marie Mianowski. "Introduction | Thresholds and Refuges: Hospitality as a Challenge." *ILCEA. Revue de l'Institut Des Langues et Cultures d'Europe, Amérique, Afrique, Asie et Australie,* no. 50 (1 March 2023). https://doi.org/10.4000/ilcea.16139.

Korody, Nicholas. "Intimate Distance: The Technosexual Architecture of Camming." *E-Flux* (blog), October 2019. https://www.e-flux.com/architecture/positions/280819.

Malavasi, Rachele, and Almo Farina. "Neighbours Talk: Interspecific Choruses among Songbirds." *Bioacoustics 22,* no. 1 (12 August 2012): 33–48.

McKibben, Bill. "Racism, Police Violence, and the Climate Are Not Separate Issues." *The New Yorker,* 4 June 2020.

Osten, Marion von. "Swooping in and out of the Tiniest Niches on the Facade." In *Making Futures,* edited by Markus Bader, Rosario Talevi, Tatjana Schneider, Juan Chacón, George Kafka, Anna Kokalanova, and Christof Mayer, xx–xx. Spector Books, 2022.

Ortega, Mariana. *In-Between: Latina Feminist Phenomenology, Multiplicity, and the Self.* State University of New York Press, 2016.

Pekowsky, Sophia. "Postpartum as Portal: Reimagining Western Conceptions of the Human Through Linocut Printmaking Workshops on Postpartum and Motherhood." 2022. https://studenttheses.uu.nl/handle/20.500.12932/42724.

Petti, Alessandro. "Refugee Heritage. The Architecture of Exile IV. B." *E-Flux* (blog), February 2017. https://www.e-flux.com/architecture/refugee-heritage/99756/the-architecture-of-exile-iv-b/.

Shildrick, Margrit. *Embodying the Monster: Encounters with the Vulnerable Self.* SAGE Publications, 2002. https://doi.org/10.4135/9781446220573.

Singh, Ashika. "Towards Dwelling in Spaces of Inhospitality: A Phenomenological Exploration of Home in Nahr Al-Barid." In *Making Home(s) in Displacement,* edited by Ashika Singh, Luce Beeckmans, Alessandra Gola, and Hilde Heynen, 61–82. Leuven University Press, 2022.

Szczesiul, Anthony. *The Southern Hospitality Myth. Ethics, Politics, Race, and American Memory.* University of Georgia Press, 2017. https://ugapress.org/book/9780820332765/the-southern-hospitality-myth.

TallBear, Kim. "Making Love and Relations Beyond Settler Sex and Family." In *Making Kin Not Population,* edited by Adele Clarke and Donna J. Haraway, 145–64. Prickly Paradigm Press, 2018.

Tsing, Anna Lowenhaupt. "From the Margins." *Cultural Anthropology* 9, no. 3 (1994): 279–97.

Tsing, Anna Lowenhaupt. *The Mushroom at the End of the World: On the Possibility of Life in Capitalist Ruins.* Princeton University Press, 2015.

workshops

Costanza-Chock, Sasha. *Design Justice: Community-Led Practices to Build the Worlds We Need.* MIT Press, 2020.

hooks, bell. *Teaching Critical Thinking.* Routledge, 2010.

COLOPHON

Set Margins' Number 80

They Asked Me to Design a House, I Asked Them to Design a Home.
Beyond the Architectural House. Reflections and Exercises on Domestic Life.

Ilaria Palmieri & Georgina Pantazopoulou (Eds.)

ISBN: 9 789083 532578

Editors: Ilaria Palmieri,
Georgina Pantazopoulou

Contributing authors: Noemi Biasetton, Ramón Jiménez Cárdenas, Cecilia Casabona, Panos Dragonas, Edit Collective, Davide Tommaso Ferrando, Ines Glowania, Platon Issaias, Nicholas Korody, la-di-da, Kevin Shu LAI, Rising Lai, Setareh Noorani, Ilaria Palmieri, Georgina Pantazopoulou, Sophia Pekowsky, Michele Rinaldi, Valentina Rizzi, Vida Rucli, Lara Schrijver, Susanna Tomassini, Feven Gebeyehu Zeru.

Illustrations: Georgina Pantazopoulou

Graphic design: Georgina Pantazopoulou, Elisa Piazzi

Text editor: Noemi Biasetton,
Anna Karampela, Ilaria Palmieri

Proofreader: Anna Karampela

Advisor: Freek Lomme / Set Margins'

Fonts: Artusi, Compagnon

Printer: BALTO print, Kaunas

Papers: Perigraphica 90grams & 240grams, MELO 60 grams

This publication is made with the generous support from the Graham Foundation for Advanced Studies in the Fine Arts (US) and Stimuleringsfonds (NL)

First edition: 1500 copies, 2025

Set Margins'
www.setmargins.press

Graham Foundation

creative industries fund NL